"OXFORD 5904S."

"WINDRUSH"
DAVENANT ROAD,
OXFORD.

Feb. 7 1957

Dear Mr Padfield,

Many thanks for your letter. Good — that's settled. You have a place. If anyone you know, by the way, is thinking of volunteering for the <u>Mayflower</u>, please tell them she's full. All we need is a good cook now.

Sincerely yours

MAYFLOWER II DIARY

Sketches from a
Lost Age

Peter Padfield

CASA FORTE
PRESS

ACKNOWLEDGEMENTS

I had to be persuaded to publish this diary and my sketches made on *Mayflower II's* 1957 voyage. The chief whips were my son Guy and his two sisters, and John Symes, a sailing man, who persisted in reminding us it must be done. Marietta Mullen and John Kemp of the 50-50 Club were equally encouraging. I am grateful to these persuaders, for as the book has taken shape I have grown to love it as a vivid reminder of a splendid crew and a youthful, so hopeful time – which I doubt now can ever be recreated.

I took with me on the voyage an 8 mm cine camera, several reels of Kodachrome film, a 35 mm Kodak Retina camera for still photos, a sketch book containing 30 leaves of 'Best Cartridge Paper', and assorted pencils – although not, it seems, a rubber! Guy has integrated frames from the cine – unfortunately grainy, but we believe historic quality as a record of the voyage trumps picture quality – together with my still photos and sketches into the four letters I sent home to my mother to preserve as a diary of the voyage.

It is difficult at this distance in time to assert that all photos reproduced here were frames from my cine film or stills from my camera, but I believe they were – except for the crew photo taken at Brixham (p.107), which was undoubtedly the work of the *Life* magazine photographer, the late Gordon Tenney. I have tried but failed to locate the curator of his archive. Apart from that one photo I believe all other illustrations are my own work, or taken with my camera, and have never been published before, except some in my own book, *The Sea is a Magic Carpet*.

Finally, I should like to acknowledge my debt to Guy for his enthusiasm, dedication and technical digital talents in bringing this book to press, to Helena Cavendish de Moura for her leap of faith in acquiring it for her publishing house, to Ellie Donovan of Plimoth Plantation for her enthusiastic welcome for this book, and to all at the Plantation over the past years for lavish generosity and hospitality during the reunions of the 1957 *Mayflower* crew.

BOOKS BY PETER PADFIELD

BIOGRAPHY
Dönitz: The Last Führer
Himmler: Reichsführer-SS
Hess: Flight for the Führer
(in paperback, *Hess: The Führer's Disciple*)
Hess, Hitler & Churchill

NAVAL AND MARITIME HISTORY
The Sea is a Magic Carpet
The Titanic and the Californian
An Agony of Collisions
Aim Straight: A Biography of Admiral Sir Percy Scott
Broke and the Shannon: A Biography of Admiral Sir Philip Broke
The Battleship Era (in paperback, *Battleship*)
Guns at Sea: A History of Naval Gunnery
The Great Naval Race: Anglo-German rivalry, 1900-1914
Nelson's War
Tide of Empires: Decisive Naval Campaigns in the Rise of the West
Vol. I: 1481-1654
Vol. II: 1654-1763
Rule Britannia: The Victorian and Edwardian Navy
Beneath the Houseflag of the P & O: A Social History
Armada: A Celebration of the 400ᵗʰ Anniversary of the Defeat of the
Spanish Armada
War Beneath the Sea: Submarine Conflict 1939-1945
Maritime Supremacy and the Opening of the Western Mind
Maritime Power and the Struggle for Freedom
Maritime Dominion and the Triumph of the Free World

(AS CONTRIBUTOR)
The Trafalgar Companion (ed. Alexander Stilwell)
Dreadnought to Daring (ed. Peter Hore)

NOVELS
The Lion's Claw
The Unquiet Gods
Gold Chains of Empire
Salt and Steel

DEDICATED
to the crew who sailed Mayflower II
from Plymouth, Devon, to Plymouth,
Massachusetts in 1957 to replicate the
original voyage of the Pilgrim Fathers
in 1620 and reinforce their legacy
of freedom, trade, kinship and hope

To
Commander Alan Villiers DSC
(who selected this excellent band)
Warwick Charlton
(who inspired the venture and saw it through)
Stuart Upham
(Master Ship-builder)

Godfrey Wicksteed, 1st Mate
Adrian Small, 2nd Mate
Capt. Jan Junker, 3rd Mate
Ike Marsh, Bosun
Edgar Mugridge, Carpenter
Walter Godfrey, Cook

Andrew Anderson-Bell Dick Brennan
David Cauvin Charles Church
Maitland Edey (for *Life* Magazine)
Fred Edwards Mike Ford John Goddard
James Horrocks Lee Israel (photographer)
Andrew Lindsay Julian Lugrin (photographer)
Joseph Meany Graham Nunn
Joe Powell Jack Scarr Harry Sowerby
Dr. John Stevens Gordon Tenney (photographer)
David Thorpe Beric Watson
Sub Lt. John Winslow RN

The author sketching aboard Mayflower II, *1957.*

FOREWORD

The idea of building a replica of the original *Mayflower* which brought the Pilgrim Fathers to America in 1620 and sending her across the Atlantic in the track of the Pilgrim Fathers who founded the United States was conceived by the British entrepreneur, Warwick Charlton, as a way of thanking the United States for coming in on Britain's side in the Second World War. The little bark was built of British oak and Oregon pine in Brixham, Devon, by traditional methods and sailed from Plymouth, Devon, to Plymouth, Massachusetts, under the square-rig sailing captain, Alan Villiers, in 1957.

One of those fortunate enough to secure a place in the crew was Peter Padfield. This book is his diary of the voyage exactly as he wrote it on board, illustrated with his own pencil sketches of sails, rigging and crew members, together with frames from a cine film he made during the voyage.

Peter Padfield has since become a leading naval historian. His diary here is written with the passion and descriptive flair that have brought him to prominence. He won the Mountbatten Maritime Prize in 2003 for the second volume of his *Maritime Supremacy* trilogy. The first volume is listed in Professor James R. Holmes' (U.S. Naval War College) 'all-time top ten books about the sea', and won universal praise:

'...this lucid, passionately argued and beautifully written history ranks among the finest of recent times', Saul David, *The Sunday Times*

'Coming from one of Britain's leading historians *Maritime Supremacy* presents a mighty thesis: that all civil liberties essentially derive from sea power', N.A.M Rodger, *The Times Literary Supplement*

'Peter Padfield is the best British naval historian of his generation now working', John Keegan, *Daily Telegraph* (on *War Beneath the Sea*)

CONTENTS

INTRODUCTION

WHEN a hapless reporter from the *Daily Mail* had the temerity to give *Mayflower II* a 50/50 chance of reaching America, the crew threw a sack over him, bound him to the fo'c'sle doorpost and doused him with dishwater. Whatever the objective odds, this was not an adventure to be undertaken by halves. Like *Mayflower* before her, *Mayflower II* set sail for the New World on a flood tide of hope and with a following wind of exuberant confidence quite overriding any doubts and fears the crew might privately have harboured. Thus was born, with a gesture of mocking defiance, the 50/50 Club.

The past cannot truly be understood without awareness that when it was lived it was the cusp of the future. Where we look back on a well rehearsed, irreversible chain of cause and effect, the actors of history looked forward into a vast ocean of possibility, bounded only by an ever-receding horizon. To see why they did what they did and thought what they thought you need to be there with them, if not in fact, then in imagination. The *Mayflower II* project was conceived in just such a spirit: of reliving, in fact as well as imagination, the incredible voyage of the Pilgrim Fathers. So far as was humanly possible, everything was engineered to be as it would have been over three centuries before. There were no safety harnesses, no following squadron of backup vessels, no airlifts of supplies, no radar and only the wind for power. The one concession to modernity was a radio, run off a small diesel engine. Captain Villiers and his crew sailed by the stars and the angle of the noonday sun, judging sea and wind by ancient skills passed down through generations of seafaring tradition. Without a doubt it would be impossible – illegal – to do the same thing today. The risks were as real for the adventurers of 1957 as they were for the Pilgrim Fathers of 1620.

It is in something of the same spirit that this book too is offered. Not as a retrospective, reminiscence or memoir, but as a small glimpse into what it was like to be there, through the unedited diary, sketches and cine film of one of the crew. It is not so much a book about the voyage as a fragment or relic of it, unaltered since my father came ashore. That is why, despite his protestations, my father's family and friends urged him to publish. He feared this was little more than an exercise in self-indulgence and that his record had no merit or interest except to him. That, surely, is for others to judge. As one by one the original players in this great fancy dress adventure creep silently to their rest, it would seem unthinkable to let these captured memories die too, or languish in some forgotten suitcase.

My father earned his berth on *Mayflower II* when he was 25. Ahead of him lay not just the vast expanse of the Atlantic Ocean but life itself, with all its unpredictable currents and tides, storms and windless calms. Since that day he has travelled the world, married and raised a family, run a business and published more than thirty books about maritime history and latterly the Third Reich. Most recently, after 58 years journeying together, he lost his beloved wife and fellow adventurer, my mother. He is an older, wiser and much less innocent man than the eager youth who jumped at the chance of spending a couple of months in 16th century conditions of hard labour aboard a tall ship. His studies of the darkest sides of human nature, in concentration camps, vivisection laboratories and intensive farms, have left their irreversible mark, casting doubt over old certainties and challenging previously unchallenged assumptions. Had he known in 1957 what he knows now, this document would be a very different kind of record with a very different commentary. And of course, if the Pilgrim Fathers of 1620 had known what we know now, theirs would have been a very different voyage, to what would have become a very different land.

But such counterfactuals are irrelevant. History is what it is, we were what we were and we have become what we have become. The only thing we can change is the future, learning, we hope, from the past. And whether there remains to us an ocean to cross or one final paddle to the far shore, we must put to sea with unreserved courage, hope and joy. If any naysayer should dare suggest we have only a 50/50 chance of making it to our New World, we know what to do with him!

To the 50/50 Club!

Guy Padfield

Woodbridge, Suffolk, May 2019

LETTER I

7th April – 25th April

1957

LETTER I

at Moorings,
River Dart,
Devon

Please stow this in a large
box very carefully as it is
the only diary type document
I possess.

Dear Mum,

I am starting to write to you now as much for the record as
anything else. In fact I will try and keep it up as a sort of diary –
if I get the time for peaceful thought etc. Don't read it if you
don't want to, but you might keep it.

Sunday April 7th

Left home at 8.30, if times mean anything, for the long journey
down to Brixham. Left the train from Paddington at Churston
and travelled in a taxi from there to Brixham in company with an
astonishingly tall photographer from *Life* Magazine (the first
syllable stressed) and his baggage. Arriving at Brixham I was
detailed by the local representatives of the *Mayflower* Project to
the St Kilda boarding house where I met Anderson Bell, the Scot
from Addis Abbaba whom I had first met at the Press
Conference three weeks back, Andy Lindsay, an American trying
to get a berth on the *Mayflower* in view of his previous time under
Villiers in the *Joseph Conrad*, Charlie Church, a Chief P.O. from
the Royal Canadian Navy, Harry Sowerby and his wife Wendy.
The following day we were joined by Joe Powell, an ex-
commando film stunt man and Wally the cook.

I took a stroll around the town and up to the cliffs overlooking the harbour in the evening, and was very impressed with the lines of the little ship three dimensional in the water, after the various pictures I had seen.

Monday April 8th - Sunday 14th

Walking down to the quay every morning we would wait in a shivering group for the boat to take us out to *Mayflower* where we worked like slaves on occasions, loading and stowing ballast and then treasure chests from the yard, and also stores for the voyage. We took sandwiches at lunchtime to the 'Ship' cafe and then often worked till six or seven in the evening when we would have a hearty meal and cheerful discussion at the digs. Mr and Mrs Franklin were the most considerate and thoughtful hosts. On leaving we presented them with a large box of chocolates and plan to give them a signed picture of the ship under way when we arrive in America.

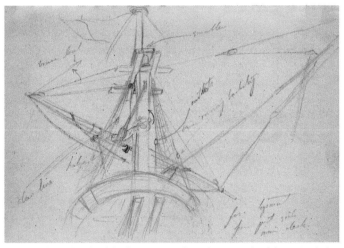

The author's sketch of the fore topmast from the port side of the main deck; note footrope running below yard.

On Friday we broke out all the sails for the first time and caused a lot of excitement on shore, where 200 phone calls poured into the Office asking if *Mayflower* was about to sail. I had my first taste of handling the braces and running rigging and then furling the topsail, which scared me no end as Joe Powell's seventeen stone bore down on the footropes and perched me right up almost over the yard on the outboard side where I had one foot and one knee hooked into the rope.

On Sunday we worked very late trying to stow all the treasure chests, which, however we did not accomplish, and had great expectations of sailing on Monday, the day we were due to sail from Plymouth.

Monday 15th April

We brought our gear down to the quay in a taxi and stowed it aboard, and then loaded the remaining treasure chests. We had our first meal aboard the ship and found it excellently cooked. There was no sign of sailing though, and the Doctor, Fred Edwards, Mike Ford and David Thorpe and myself went for a practice pull in the gig that the Doctor had borrowed from Paignton sea rangers for rowing Alan Villiers ashore in

Loading 'treasure chests' of British manufactured goods.

Plymouth. We later repaired to the yacht club with the intention of either borrowing or stealing their ceremonial boathook.

However they very obligingly let us have it, and also made great efforts to secure us another oar for our gig, David Thorpe having broken one in the first few minutes. I learned the local gambling game called 'spouf' and lost a round of drinks.

I remember an amusing incident that happened on Saturday, when Anderson-Bell – known usually as Scotty – met a girl-friend of his on the quay just as we were about to put out to the ship. We catcalled him and yelled, and he came to sit in the boat, but jumped out just as we pushed off, and made towards the town in search of the girl. She meanwhile had walked around to the outer quay to have a better look at *Mayflower* with two of her friends, and as we passed in the motor boat we saw them standing at the end of the quay. We put in again and hauled them aboard rapidly – although I think they were rather disconcerted at being shanghaid for no apparent reason by a bunch of piratical-looking sailors – we all sported colourful headgear and clothes – and then took them out to the ship, leaving Scotty vainly searching the town for them. When he finally appeared trying to get aboard, and not knowing that his girlfriend was aboard, he was met with an array of sticks and boathooks and not allowed to come up the ladder. Then he spotted the girls. It was all beautifully timed.

In the morning there was a short break in the work of the ship while about eight of the crew seized the Daily Mail reporter shortly after he boarded, bound him to the fo'c'sle head, put a sack over his head and anointed him with dirty dish water. This was in retaliation for a derogatory and unseamanlike article he had written giving the *Mayflower* a 50/50 chance of reaching New Plymouth. He took it very well and made quite a story out of it the next day.

I have never seen so many photographers and reporters as have besieged us all the time in Brixham. They are everywhere all the time interrupting the work to ask 'just hold that position a moment please boys' – 'now will you get together in a group about here' – 'Look as if you're talking to each other' – and so on. We also sign our autographs regularly several times a day.

Tying the Daily Mail reporter to a fo'c'sle doorpost. 'Doc' Stevens in the lead, John Winslow behind.

John Winslow, the Fleet Air Arm sub-lieutenant, is the most photographed and publicised member of the crew at the moment, and the latest 'scoop' is his growing only half a beard for a £50 bet.

Tuesday 16th April

Waiting around expecting to sail, we heard rumours flying around which eventually crystallised into the fact that there was a legal tussle in London about handing over the ship. Everyone was very fed up about it, especially as the shore was lined with hundreds of expectant people, and the harbour was full of boats and launches circling us and waiting for the big moment.

At about four-thirty, however, Villiers at last persuaded the powers that be that we should go out for a trial run. We were towed a few cables out from the breakwater and then broke out the sails, ending with the spritsail and then the lateen. We were followed by hooting craft crowded to a dangerous list with photographers and sightseers, and circled by low planes all the time. Several shots were fired. Villiers called me to the wheel and

7

l took it for her first run to sea. She seemed to sail very nicely at about five knots and really felt like a ship.

The author at the wheel.

We were all very pleased with her performance I think, especially the builder, Upham, and the designer, Baker, who took the wheel for a long time coming home. We tied up at about eight o'clock and I was up on the main topyard furling the topsail. The photographers in the watching launches all seemed to think we were a grand sight, and the following morning's papers all had front page pictures.

Wednesday 17th April

A rather gloomy morning with nothing much to do and plenty of rumours flying around that we wouldn't sail that day because of those 'lawyers up in London'. At about 4.30 news trickled

through that we were sailing to Dartmouth and at 4.47 we were towed out of Brixham for the last time, and all the way around to Dartmouth, where we were greeted with the usual guns, launches, cheering crowds and low aeroplanes as we moored to buoys. One caustic sailor-man tying us up yelled out "What – have you come all the way from Brixham?"

Waiting to sail: Edgar Mugridge (left) and Dick Brennan.

I developed a cold, which I had felt the previous day as we were towed in a cold S.W'ly force 5.

Thursday 18th April

Ashore in the pram for shopping in the morning, followed by a practice pull in the gig to the yacht club, where the Doctor, Mike Ford, Dave Thorpe, Harry Sowerby, Fred Edwards and myself signed our name in the book and some of us had a hair wash. Later there were rumours that we were being towed out at 7.00 p.m., but when the *Englishman* appeared she moored, and we settled in for another night aboard.

Friday 19th April

Up at 4.00 a.m. for the watch, but we didn't move until about 7.00, and then we battered against a fresh headwind and head seas so much that the hawse pipes which had been left unplugged took the seas green, and most of us got soaked to the skin trying to ram canvas and fenders into the openings. The water swirled ankle deep amidships in the 'tween decks and very soon all hands were baling with dustpans and buckets. I surveyed them from a hammock feeling that I had done my bit in getting soaked to the skin beforehand, but couldn't hold out for very long against the hints, and started dishing dirty water into relays of buckets brought by Sir Alan Moore,[1] who had been sleeping under my hammock the previous night.

He is a very interesting old boy, very nearly 80, an authority on medieval ships and rigging who shows a very active interest in this rigging and has been leaping around the yards furling sails and taking photographs with a box 'Brownie' which he pulls from an old canvas kit bag.

Soon after midday we arrived off Drake Island [Plymouth] with an armada of small craft overflowing with people as it was a beautiful day. We started loading treasure chests and the rest of the stores almost immediately from a lighter, and worked almost continuously until half past five. I had a break when Uncle Bertie,[11] Nim, Willie and Lois together with Allan, Sandra, their two boys and a couple of guests arrived in the Chief of Staff's pinnace, delivered us a set of scrubbed oars, which I had asked for from Dartmouth (after Harry Sowerby had cracked two in succession at the practice) and then came aboard for a quick look around.

[1] *Author of* The Last Days of Mast and Sail
[11] *My uncle, Bertie, captain of the cruiser,* H.M.S. Cumberland, *was married to Naomi ('Nim') and they had two children, William and Lois. Allan Trewby was a cousin.*

The Chief of Staff pinnace.

In the evening I had a luxurious bath at Bertie's Hotel, the *Strathmore*,[1] followed by a good dinner, sherry, beer, and then we went to Allan and Sandra's house and had a few whiskies. She is a fascinating woman, still very attractive, and they have two very well-behaved little boys and a nice large house. He is apparently a great brain and is at the moment principal of the Engineering College there. I was quite lionised throughout, to which I have not yet got used. After a good night's sleep, the first out of my hammock for some nights, I caught a fisherman back to the ship the following morning.

Saturday 20th April

Aboard there was a great congregation of pressmen and photographers and cameras flashed in every direction as the crew

---

[1] *An extraordinary coincidence since it was from the wardroom of the P & O liner,* Strathmore, *that I had first written to Alan Villiers applying for a berth aboard* Mayflower.

were ordered to change into 'fancy dress' before 9.00 a.m. The gig's crew, in which 'Scotty' had relieved Harry Sowerby in the bow went for a practice pull, and were then towed behind the Lord Mayor's launch to a position near the *Mayflower* steps, where Alan Villiers and Warwick Charlton transferred to the gig and we pulled them to the steps in fine style. There followed a civic and partly religious ceremony at which Villiers made a fighting speech – quotes: 'New ships are never on time – like brides – But they're good when you get them – (*sotto voce* – sometimes). I have read some arrant nonsense in the papers about the *Mayflower* having a 50/50 chance of making it. Have we forgotten our seafaring tradition? It was little ships like this

Mayflower II *moored at Plymouth, Devon.*

coming many times from the ports of Devon and Cornwall that founded the Commonwealth – not blooming great liners' – 'I have a splendid ship and an excellent crew' – etc. etc. We all had a sip of sherry from a silver loving cup and then rowed Villiers and the Lord Mayor of Plymouth back towards the ship. However we were overtaken by the Lord Mayor's boat after some way, and had to transfer our important cargo. We all thought this was pointless and undignified, for although the ship was a long way away we felt we should complete the task. The pulling was reckoned very good though, and we were rewarded with a bottle of Champagne from the 'Old Man' on Easter Sunday, which was drunk with pomp and ceremony before a couple of the photographers who had about a dozen cameras between them.

The gig's crew. Standing, from left: Fred Edwards, 'Scotty' Anderson-Bell, Mike Ford (and Felix the kitten), Peter Padfield. Seated: 'Doc' Stevens, David Thorpe.

After returning to the ship we got a tow back to *H.M.S. Cumberland*, and I enquired after Bertie but learned he was on Easter weekend. We were invited to the Wardroom by the Officer of the Watch and fairly plied with drink for an hour or so before we had to get back to the ship. Willie and Lois arrived just before we left and said that Bertie was coming on later, but we couldn't wait, and leaving the gig and oars in charge of the lieutenant, we repaired very merry to *Mayflower* in one of

Cumberland's boats. We were circled by the usual armada in the afternoon, and the Hoe was literally massed with bodies, colourful specks to us watching and waiting to go.

The morning had been dull and the ceremony spoiled by drizzle, but the afternoon was beautiful, and it was a very colourful sight as we slipped our moorings at five o'clock and glided out behind a small tug followed and accompanied by hordes of small dinghies, yachts, motor boats, Naval and R.A.F. pinnaces and Uncle Bertie and family and guests in his pinnace. Unfortunately the wind was very light and in the West and the tow was almost to the Eddystone Light with the result that very few of the boats were there to see us hoist (or rather drop) the sails.⚓ We made a Southerly course for the offing and later that night found variable Easterly winds which took us 15 miles East of the Eddystone by the following morning.

Sunday 21st April

After being used to dropping lights behind one at a steady 15 knots or more it is rather disconcerting to come on watch in the morning and find the same lighthouse as last night in approximately the same position. We are on doubled watches, four on and four off and sleep is difficult to come by in sufficient quantities. A reporter came aboard from a white launch early in the morning and watched us at our tasks of making anti-chafing gear. He disappeared with some letters to post and then we were visited by aeroplanes and coastal vessels, some of whom circled us several times as if in complete astonishment before making off. On occasions the reality suddenly strikes one, the absurd situation as crew of an antique looking vessel over three centuries out of date calmly sailing the waters of the channel as if it were the most natural thing in the world.

⚓ *The square sails were set by releasing the gaskets which held them to their yard, allowing them to drop, then restraining the canvas with the tacks and sheets, and angling the yard to the wind with the braces.*

A beautiful day – no wind though – and the sea held an oily smoothness as we drifted helplessly, and sometimes sternfirst with the sails continually flapping against the mast. All hands were out on deck enjoying the weather, and the skiffle group (so far Beric Watson, John Winslow, Joe Lacey, Lee Israel, and sometimes Graham Nunn) had their first practice. Later that night a light breeze blew up from the East and we went slowly on our way rejoicing.

Monday 22nd April

Easter Monday, and we continued work on the anti-chafe mats and ropes (baggywrinkle). The wind freshened a bit and we felt we were on our way. The ship started moving around as we got the swell in from the Irish Sea and various people, myself included, began to go very green about the gills and slip tablets into their mouths unobtrusively. I kept off the tablets trying to fight the awful feeling in the pit of my stomach and buzzing in my head. Below decks there is stygian blackness, and up for'd where my hammock is slung, a strong smell of tarred rope which I find very disagreeable and sick-making. The messing arrangements on the scrubbed table in the after part of the 'tween decks are very primitive and people are getting a bit fed up with the lack of organisation from the galley now, although when we first started living aboard it was great fun to be really uncivilised and stretch out right across the table to eat three courses on one plate. The novelty has worn off though, and besides we are in terrible haste to grab our food and get to sleep or on watch. There is a bare minimum of fresh water, and all the dishes and cutlery are cleaned in salt water and 'teepol' (a special detergent for sea water). There is just one bucket of this stuff and the last plates to be washed are merely smeared with an even layer of grease and then wiped with an extraordinarily filthy cloth. There are only about thirty of us. One can't begin to appreciate the hardships on the original voyage with 160, especially as we haven't really had any heavy weather yet.

The wind was force 3-4 and has freshened to 4-5 and we are busting along in fine style on a W by S course.

15

The 2nd Mate on the quarterdeck; lateen sail full of wind.

Tuesday 23rd April

Still on the 4 on, 4 off watch system – still busting through the waves at what looks to be about 8 knots, but actually averaged 4.6. David Thorpe very ill with the continued motion of the ship and I don't feel much better myself. There is a lot of talk about going the Southabout route if the wind holds in the North. At about 7 o'clock the rumour was confirmed as we squared the yards up and set a S'ly course. Great rejoicing about this as the weather is very cold and no one was looking forward to the frozen North. It is said that Villiers was partly influenced in his choice by the fact that the ship had had no trials. She is going great guns now with the wind on the starboard quarter and the yards almost square. We are standing a three watch system now which is another cause for rejoicing after the general chaos and sleeplessness of 4 on and 4 off, so we broke a bottle of rum open in the Bosun's cabin – it being his birthday – and were photographed drinking it in the fo'c'sle among the tarred coils of rope and the hammers and marline spikes by one of the *Life* photographers. Our watch consists of the Bosun, Ike Marsh, with Joe Lacey, Beric Watson, Fred Edwards, Graham Nunn, Maitland Edey and myself.

Maitland, the Assistant Editor for *Life* started on watches today and after his trick at the wheel he handed over to Joe Lacey with the words, "I don't know what you call the course but it's this one here," (pointing to one of the points on the compass card). Joe Lacey, in between singing his Irish songs was repeating this to all and sundry for the rest of the evening.

Wednesday 24th April

Still busting along, pushing tons of white foam out in a great bluff bow wave. Logging 8 knots in a force 5-6 wind, running right before it down to the S.W.

Thursday 25th April

Busting along before a rising swell and a strong breeze in brilliant sunlight. It is ideal weather for photography, and I spent hours up in the topmast shrouds manoeuvring the camera awkwardly as the shrouds jerked and pulled this way and that. They are very slack due to the dry weather.

In the afternoon we lazed in the sunshine reading and chatting while the 12-4 watch made baggywrinkle. We will be making it in our sleep soon. By 5 o'clock the wind was getting up and the swell mounting to tremendous proportions, and Villiers yelled for the topsails to be taken in and furled, which we did with great haste and treading in each other's way. Meanwhile Gordon, the *Life* photographer, contorted himself into the most extraordinary positions as he snapped hundreds of photos of the emergency.

Up the futtocks into the fore top.

Finally I went up to furl the fore topsail with Maitland and the cabin boy, Graham Nunn. I had to do most of the work as they had not done the job before, and I quite forgot to be scared stiff as I had imagined that I would be whenever I had thought about it previously. I found it quite exhilarating up there swaying wildly, hanging on to the best available rope with the wind whistling about your face and clothes. Then a quick meal grab – grab – grab over the table (if you remember any form of manners in the messroom you just don't get anything to eat) and so to the wheel and a brief talk about the slackness of the rigging with Villiers. He said it was a fine, healthy life, and I felt inclined to agree with him now that all traces of the terrible nausea in my stomach and head have at last worn off.

On deck it's fine fresh, exhilarating with the magnificent, beautiful curves of the white sails stretching overhead, and the breeze and the sun and the sea foaming past, and the little ship tugging to get ahead – but below it's like the black hole of Calcutta. One gropes one's way in pitch darkness through the cluttered and musty deck banging into things as the vessel lurches. And all the time there is the – to my mind – awful smell of tarred rope.

Mike Ford

Making
Baggywrinkle

Dave Thorpe

On our way!

LETTER II

26th April – 13th May

1957

The author's hammock below decks.

LETTER II

Friday 26th April

Out on deck at 4.00 a.m. after a night of really terrific rolling. The 'Old Man' described the motion of this vessel later in the day as typical of a Cape Horner. In my hammock though I spent a remarkably peaceful night, awakened only by the clatter and muffled lights of the watch being called at midnight. When the sun rose and we had finished washing down the scene was grand. There was a majesty and sweep of the advancing white foam-capped, blue green waves that reminded me of the remoteness of the Swiss mountains, and the coldness and cleanness of the Swiss mountains. I experienced the intense awareness of being alive that I felt on a keen Swiss morning, and the ship rolled like a hurdy-gurdy.

Later in the morning, however, came disillusion. Down in the ghastly 'tween deck the Doctor, Dave Cauvin and myself swept and scrubbed the floors and mess-table in the 50/50 club (our name for the members of the crew – given a 50/50 chance of reaching the other side by the *Daily Mail* reporter). Gordon, the *Life* photographer, took about a dozen snaps of me sweeping the 'tween decks and leaning against the tremendous rolls. There were some amusing incidents over breakfast as plates, crockery and fried eggs lurched from one side of the table, over wooden partitions, and into people's laps. Fred Edwards from Liverpool, our resident comedian, got a jug of tea over his stomach as he lay full length on the surrounding seat. It had come from the other side of the table. Several more people were sick. So far I have been very lucky.

In the afternoon watch I went out along the main yard to clear the martinets, and was again surprised at the simplicity with which one tackles a job when one has to, forgetting to be at all frightened of the swaying of the yard and the strong breeze. Joe

Lacey, a little Irish A.B. who worked as an extra in 'Moby Dick'[1] jumps around like a cat in the rigging, thoroughly at home and loving every minute of it. Yesterday, as he furled the Main topsail he was yelling and cursing at the top of his voice for the sheer joy of being up there on the swinging top. He spends most of the time when not working singing, which prompted Andy, the American from the *Joseph Conrad*[11] to remark that every ship one goes to has an Irish tenor. I replied that he was in our watch and we were going to keep him.

... busting along, main topsail full of wind.

The wind is still from the North-East and has died down from force 8 this morning to about 6 now, and the swell is slightly less confused. At about 4.30 we set the main topsail, and she's busting

[1] *The 1956 film based on Herman Melville's whaling classic. Both Joe Lacey and Joe Powell worked on the square-rigger representing the Pequod, commanded by Alan Villiers.*
[11] *A square-rigger which Villiers saved from scrap in 1937 and sailed round the world with a youthful amateur crew in a pioneering sail-training venture, not to train youngsters for the sea, but as Villiers put it, for life.*

along, rocking her lee gun'l under at times. Villiers has sent a cable to Boston giving an E.T.A. for June 7th. Today we did 155 miles, which makes our average since we left about 110 miles a day, including the day we only made 15 miles.

Saturday 27th April

Still rolling like a mad thing, still pushing through a heavy swell, still stinking in the 'tween decks. Squally in the afternoon. Furled main topsail at 19.30. The Doctor, coming out on deck to throw slops over the side, found himself up the topmast.

Sunday 28th April

Cameras clicked and the cine film rolled as Villiers dressed in uniform and medals delivered the short Sunday prayers, and then explained the second Chapter in the story of the original *Mayflower* and *Speedwell* as he did last Sunday. The Harwich Yacht Club burgee flew from the foremast, the Chicago Adventurers flag from the main, and the Red Ensign from the mizzen. The watches were changed, and we started on the 'graveyard' or 12-4.

Villiers, extreme right, photographs the crew in their pilgrim costumes.

Tuesday 30th April

This was the first day of real sunbathing. Shorts and bathing costumes were broken out, and white skins, albeit somewhat grubby, were aired in the breeze. Mait Edey, who is the only 'gentleman' – or non-mariner – to have stayed on watches with us, the rest having dropped out after the first few days, had a complete bath from a bucket. Gordon Tenney wasted several rolls of film on people shaving with sea-water, and a lot of shots of myself washing feet.

Warwick Charlton and Fred Edwards in the boat on deck.

Everyone is talking to Warwick Charlton, the originator of the project, about the festivities the other side – almost as if we were there already – mainly, I suppose because of the tremendous progress we have been making – 150 miles a day on the average. The wind backed to the North and then N.W. and dropped appreciably in the evening and I fear this will be the last 150 for some time. It was very difficult to keep the course of SW by S and we all wondered why the yards weren't braced round more to close-haul her. As it was she was running free and we couldn't get nearer to the course than S by W½W.

Wednesday 1st May

Started well as I fell out of my hammock at about 6.0 o'clock in the morning. I was then kept awake by the hatches just above my slung hammock being opened to admit the bright sunlight.

Beric Watson, John Winslow and Warwick Charlton
'It takes a worried man to sing a worried song'.

The ship ghosted along at about 2 knots under light airs and sunbathing continued unabated. Cameras were out in force, especially the 'Old Man's' whose equipment in movies and stills rivals the professional photographers aboard. The skiffle group, whose only song consists of 'It takes a worried man to sing a worried song', set topical words to it illustrating some of the amusing features of the trip so far. One of them was John Winslow's remark to the 2nd Mate when handing over the course, "By and large, sir", instead of "Full and bye" – the other was Mait Edey's wonderful hand-over of the wheel, "I don't know what the course is but it's this diamond here," in his very dry American (Princeton) drawl.

Gordon, the photographer, seems to think we are all pseudo-adventurers aboard. So far, I must admit, with this soldiers wind from the North there has not been a lot of excitement.

Thursday 2nd May

Warwick Charlton appeared on deck in the middle of the night smoking. He is very discouraged by the lack of wind, and can't understand it at all after the week of fair wind we have just had. He seemed happier in the morning when he saw we were making about three knots – until told that we were making them in the wrong direction – S.E.

He watched me sketching in the morning and remarked on the lovely curve of the sails (they are indeed lovely – especially against the backdrop of a star-studded clear night sky) and that this was one of the shapes that we had lost in our modern world. He went on to make a very simple remark that seems devastatingly true – of which, however, I had never thought. He said that the same people who would admire the shape of the sails in my drawing – or anyone's drawing – would think them pointless and meaningless if they were presented as a picture in the abstract without the ship and the tangle of masts and shrouds to hold them in and make them real objects. He instanced the sculpture of Barbara Hepworth. He is certainly an interesting talker on most subjects, though he looks rather pale, unkempt and nightclubby.

My job on watch was to oil down the main yard, which meant clambering out to the end with an awkward can. I didn't mind it at all, but was very careful where I put my hands and feet as, although we have been at sea some time I had not been out to the end of the yard before. However I was too slow for the Mate, watching from below, who remarked to Fred Edwards that I didn't seem to like it out there. In actual fact I quite enjoyed it by the end when I had to come down and take over the wheel. While I was up there Mait Edey had got the ship 'aback' – letting the wind catch the wrong side of the sails. She soon gathered sternway and we 'weared ship' – a manoeuvre which we performed a second time later in the afternoon when the 'Old Man' told Beric Watson not to put too many turns on the wheel but to let her steer herself – result; 'aback' again.

An amusing incident was recollected in our conversation tonight about the visit to *H.M.S. Cumberland* in Plymouth. We rolled up in our 'fancy dress', and the rating on the gangway – without batting an eyelid – reported, "Six pilgrims come aboard sir," to the Officer of the deck.

The weather continues beautifully warm – although a trifle chilly at nights – and today Scotty sighted land after taking a shower from a bucket in the beak. I think he was the first to see it, although whether the O.O.W., the 2nd. Mate, who was working in the top, had seen it previously I don't know. It turned out to be Palma in the Canary Islands, and about 84 miles away. We are gradually closing it all the time, albeit the wind (about NW by N) is away from it.

Friday 3rd May

Up on deck at midnight to find ourselves pelting the wrong way, full and bye to a S.W'ly wind about force 4 straight for Tenerife. At 12.30 the 'Old Man' came on deck and we furled main and fore topsails. Hardly any other watch has touched the topsails so far. We take them off and put them on with reckless abandon, and have earned ourselves the title of 'topsail watch'. A rather amusing incident on the foretopsail when I handed the Mate the foresail clew garnet to heave on instead of the topsail clew line. He heaved away desperately for some minutes without getting anywhere before he discovered. I was sent up to the main top to furl the sail afterwards. I found trying to steer the ship 'full and bye' at night without coming up into the wind and catching her 'aback' a very tricky business.

By the time I arrived on deck in the morning the wind had backed to the N.W. and we were scudding along in the right direction again. There was a very confused swell though and bodies were flying to the rail at frequent intervals and coughing it up.

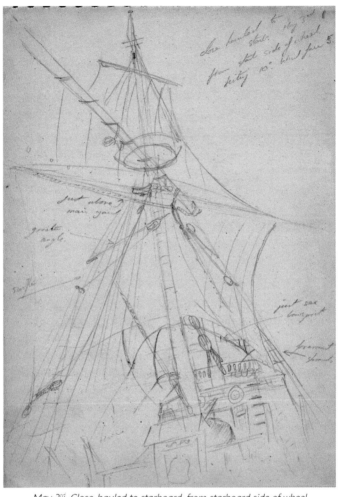

May 3rd. Close-hauled to starboard, from starboard side of wheel.

I never felt better and took full advantage of the masses of uneaten food later in the day. The cooking is still first class with plenty of variety and reasonable quantities, although jam and butter are rationed rather severely. There was much hilarity over the people who were sick, one of the loudest laughers being Joe Powell – but his turn came soon after dinner when he flew up from the saloon and discharged over the weather rail to escape everyone's notice. However he was seen and made to suffer. Even the *Joseph Conrad* veteran, Andy Lindsay was taking it in turns with the Doctor to be sick in the fore top as they mended the hole in the foretopsail caused some days ago by chafing. They watched the sick flying in aerodynamic curves over the foresail to be sucked up and under the spritsail, all of which caused hilarious topics for discussion at dinner. It really is terrible up there in the tops in rough weather. The ship is so stiff it feels as if the masts are trying to shake you right off.

7th May from port-side fo'c'sle, looking aft to quarterdeck and poop.

This afternoon Beric Watson, one of the worst sufferers, walked up to take the wheel with a saucepan to be sick in clipped to his waist. The 'Old Man' seemed very amused.

Main course and main topsail from fore top.

Enough of that subject. This afternoon Joe Lacey yelled down from the fore-top, where he was working on the sail, "Land on the port beam." Villiers, standing right beneath, roared up, "It's been there all day," and Joe's head soon disappeared. In the afternoon we passed on our S.W. course between Palma to starboard and Teneriffe and Gomera to port. Teneriffe stuck up grandly above the piled white cumulus clouds abeam, and had a little cap of white snow on the top. It looked very impressively high. In no time at all we were abeam of Gomera and passed – I should estimate – about ten miles off. It seemed to inspire both the American *Life* men to want to come back and visit the Canaries at their leisure – why? I don't know, as the island looked very rugged, precipitous and misty against the glaring clearness of the day and the bright blue sea. In the evening we altered to the Southard to pass under the lee of Ferra, which was right ahead of our course.

At the wheel this afternoon I appreciated – really for the first time, I suppose – just how lucky I was to have secured a berth on *Mayflower*. The sails curving beautifully away ahead and the little ship listing over ten degrees with the weight of wind, and the white foam creaming out in a tremendously broad blanket as she rams her blunt bow into the swell, and the bright sunlight, and the keen wind and the good company aboard. What more can you ask for – especially when you can laugh at the procession of figures leaning hard over the rail – laugh with a steady stomach – but then I haven't been up aloft today. My nose has burned and peeled badly and is smeared white with some zinc ointment that Charlie Church provided.

Saturday 4th May

We spliced the mainbrace with 'Old Navy Rum' to celebrate finding the N.E. Trades. They blew steadily from the N.N.E.

Sunday 5th May

Wind N.E. – sailing smoothly at about 5 knots. We all dressed up in 'fancy dress' at 10 o'clock and gathered on the quarterdeck for prayers, but mainly for the photographers, who had a field day – especially with the 1st Mate, who lapped it up – as always – and kept his rig on until 4.0 o'clock.

I felt quite exhausted from my week on the 12-4 with little sleep – and today was 'Peggy', which consists of serving the food at meals, washing up afterwards, scrubbing the table and stairs,

David Cauvin, and Godfrey Wicksteed, 1ˢᵗ Mate, with cross staff.

sweeping the 'tween decks and washing up the drying up cloths – all in a thick atmosphere of diesel oil with ultra-dim lighting, which is non-existent when you move a few yards for'd. There is undoubtedly no worse job aboard, and the end of 'peggying' will be my main reason for feeling happy at the end of the voyage. We were issued with sweets and cigarettes – I picked up a large tin of 'Sharps' toffee and the watches were shortened and changed, so that now we have only four, Beric Watson, Fred Edwards, Mait Edey and myself on the 8-12.

Fred Edwards, resident comedian, suggested signalling the first passenger ship we saw and asking her if the war had ended. The 'Old Man' said at prayers that we had done 1,700 miles and had 3,500 to go, which seems an elastic distance, growing bigger the more mileage we leave behind us. Fred's banns were read – as he is being married on his return to the U.K., and we all murmured "Rhubarb, rhubarb, rhubarb," discontentedly, which raised a few grins.

Monday 6th May

In the 'Ship' in Brixham Villiers told me that I was to be Mail

Officer. Today I found out just what the job entailed. In the Mail room are four sacks and four cartons filled with boxes which are pressed tight with *Mayflower* envelopes each stamped and each waiting to be franked with *Mayflower II* – Maiden Voyage.[⚓] I have to organise this and pack them up afterwards.

Working in the Post Office. Left: John Winslow; Right, Joe Meany, Jack Scarr, David Thorpe, Scotty, Mike Ford.

Tuesday 7th May

The mailing, which continued throughout the night in desultory fashion, has produced more franked envelopes than there are boxes to hold them. It is going to be a problem packing them up again and finding more boxes. I have been 'Peggy' for three consecutive mornings now – under a new system – and together with the mailing, which takes up a lot of out-of-watch time, and the violent motion the ship is doing, I am feeling lousy. I made

⚓ This was one of Warwick Charlton's wheezes for raising money for funding the *Mayflower II* project.

some sketches from the fore top today, and we had a record day's run of 160 miles. And so to watch.

Wednesday 8th May

Mailing all through the night and all this morning. I instituted a production line assembly with one person feeding envelopes to the stamper – and roped in Warwick Charlton, Stuart Upham, and the two photographers, Julian Lugrin and Lee Israel – in fact most of the afterguard who live in the Great Cabin and do sweet nothing all day – although the photographers can often be seen in odd positions with magnificently expensive pieces of equipment and encouraging jargon – "Two virile young men, please – to appear on the front page of *Life* for the great American public."

Gordon Tenney, the Life Magazine *photographer.*

As I write I can hear Edgar Mugridge, the carpenter, snoring like a traction engine, and immediately above him the block for the wire steering gear is screaming like a cow in agony. Between these two sleeps Julian on the smallest cot on the ship. All around me are sounds like a B.B.C. effects man imitating a rounding of the Horn by Magellan. There was a period of relative calm this evening and Lee Israel remarked that the best way to start her rolling again was to go to bed. It seems to have worked.

7th May – running free, wind starboard quarter.

The wind, which this morning was N.E. has veered to the East and at about 8.30 this morning we squared the yards for this shift. We are getting to know the ropes pretty well by now. The wind change brought a warm front with it and there were several groups out on deck talking quietly in the beautiful moonlit night. It has always been too cold for any prolonged sessions on deck before. I thoroughly enjoyed lying back with my head on a rubber dinghy, watching the foremast circling the clouds and listening to other people talking – and on the look-out I enjoyed, as always, hanging on the weather shrouds where they meet the futtocks going over the top and watching the little ship below ploughing through the sea for all the world like a steamer, pushing sheets of solid cream yards out ahead.

To revert to the production line stamping this morning, the two rival groups Julian and Warwick and Lee and Stuart Upham were working up a terrific speed trying to outdo each other, so that the tap of their stamps – first on the inkpad and then on the letter – took up a regular metronome rhythm. I'm afraid that some people won't get entirely legible postmarks on their letters. To round off a successful morning Lee Israel stamped his finger very hard, tore the skin and drew blood. We have now completed four sacks of mail and have six cartons to go.

Thursday 9th May

Was chiefly remarkable for the fact that I had my first bath since that wonderful night in Plymouth – and did I need it! I took two buckets up to the beak, one containing 'teepol' – a special salt water detergent – and one containing fresh sea water, and with these washed myself bit by bit, letting the various portions dry in the sun. The beak is about the warmest place in the ship as it is sheltered from the wind by the fo'c'sle, and points into the setting sun by the nature of our course.

Warwick Charlton saw the Captain about stamped envelopes for the crew this afternoon after we had badgered him about it unmercifully. As a result I was instructed to give 100 to the crew, which worked out at 3 a person.

The Doc and Dave Cauvin thought of dropping bottles over the side with messages in. Scotty duly typed them out, they were signed by all members of the crew, placed in cyder bottles and dropped overboard I think – although I didn't see the ceremony. Today was also remarkable for the first real quarrel, which

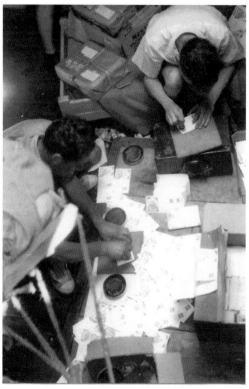

Post Office under author's hammock.

sprang up at first sitting for lunch. I was on the wheel and didn't see it, but one of the main combatants was Joe Lacey, who is always somewhat quick-tempered. I am only surprised that the trip has been remarkably free from quarrels so far – especially with the conditions we live in. The meals are a forest of hands grabbing across the mess table and greasy dishes passed around for everyone to help themselves – three courses in the same plate to save washing up. After the tiff today it was decided that someone should serve the food out onto plates instead of everyone serving themselves. This system came under fire from Harry Sowerby and the same Joe Lacey this evening at dinner, so what the upshot will be I don't know. Have just learned that the bottles did not go over the wall. All the signatures have not been collected and also it is too dark for films. Everything aboard centres around cameras – batches and batteries of them.

Looking aft at the bow from the beak head.

Looking down into the beak. The hole in the timber floor to port of the bowsprit served as the lavatory, traditionally, 'the heads'. The inscription on the left of the aperture reads, 'Officers are requested to adjust their dress before leaving.'

Friday 10th May

The constant wind has dropped and we are little more than ghosting at 3-4 knots. In the morning a pocket-handkerchief sized stunsail was hoisted on the starboard fore yard and promptly blew the wrong way. I'm sure it does no good. Fred remarked that we now had something no steamship ever had – which was a brake. In the afternoon the yards were squared for the wind which had come round to the port quarter and the stunsail filled out the right way. Three bottles were put over the side with all cameras trained on them, and at 10 o'clock the photographers had another treat when the Doctor, in surgical mask and with the tools of his trade, applied his leeches to the bare stomach of Warwick Charlton, lying full length on the main deck. The first leech, which seemed a trifle apathetic didn't bite, but the second one, applied so that our movie man could get a close-up, dug a little hole and had to be removed with salt. Otherwise another pleasant, fairly cool day – and pleasant, quiet conversation in the cool of the evening. Much discussion about tomorrow's 50/50 Club 'halfway across' dinner.

A pocket handkerchief-size stunsail was hoisted on the starboard fore yard.

Lying on my back during the watch looking up at the solid silver cotton-wool clouds with the moon and a single bright star drifting through, and the masts swaying gently – and an Irish tenor – Joe Lacey of course – baying to the night.

Saturday 11th May

Chiefly remarkable for the 'halfway' dinner in the evening at 5.30 – remarkable because the dinner fell remarkably flat. After all we had expected it proved to be the worst food (with the exception of yesterday's salt horse lunch) that we have yet experienced.

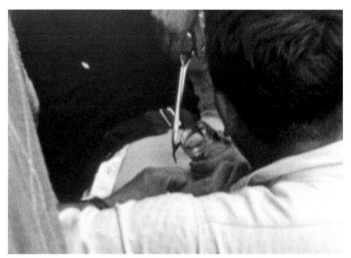

'Doc' Stevens applies leeches to Warwick Charlton's bare chest

However it was made up for by a good sing-song session on deck in the evening twilight and on into the dark with flash bulbs exploding all the time. The wind dropped later.

Sunday 12th May

We had a 'fancy dress' church parade. I clanged the bell at short intervals while the Ship's company – after stowing the cameras which had been clicking merrily – proceeded slowly up the lee ladder to the quarterdeck, which is where we now have the Sunday meetings instead of the break of the quarterdeck. The Mate held the prayer meeting while the 'Old Man' took movies from all angles. He then gave us his customary talk on the *Mayflower*'s first voyage, gave us a progress report on this voyage in which he said there were 2,700 miles to go, and the weather forecast was Easterly winds, and finally asked for 'any questions', of which there were none. This was followed by Wally, the cook, distributing Black Magic or Sharps toffee to the non-smokers and cigarettes or tobacco to the smokers. Just after breakfast the 'Old Man' had been towed in the little pram astern of the ship while he took pictures. The sails were only just filling as the wind is a light force 3.

In the afternoon Gordon and Mike Ford went overside in the pram for photographs. They cast off altogether and in no time at all were about 100 yards astern and pulling the little cockleshell madly. The crowd were laughing and waving 'Cheerio' from the deck and it seemed ages before they finally made the safety of the ship and a heaving line was thrown to them. Gordon looked white and haggard. There was not much sea but quite a long swell and the pram was full of water when she arrived back. A bit later the fore topyard snapped on the port side, and it was sent down to the deck. It was joined up again – a process known as 'fishing' – and our watch doing the last 'dog' had the task of sending her up again and setting sail after bending the rigging on. The job took the full two hours even with Ike the Bosun helping us.

The latest rumour from Warwick Charlton is that he has cabled Plymouth, Mass to ask them to send a tug to tow us in if the wind drops. The scheme is that we will appear to accept the tow with much reluctance, which is all very phoney – as most people seem to think the project itself is by now. The 'Old Man' tries to give us the right slant on the purpose of the voyage though after prayers on Sundays. He said today that it was to remind the

American people of the courage and hardihood and love of freedom of the original *Mayflower* pilgrims – all Britishers – who originated a lot that is best in the American way of life – not all, but a lot.

Trade winds; the watch below on deck, sunbathing.

Warwick Charlton is a large, ungainly man with a very white freckled skin and plenty of surplus fat with no visible muscle. He

45

moves very awkwardly still and seems to have a certain slackness about the jaws and voice, although he talks most interestingly on most topics. As the Doc remarked he has to be all things to all men – and he certainly tries hard, giving all sorts of promises which might or might not be fulfilled. The ship's company remain sceptical.

Fore top and topsail being hauled in.

Monday 13th May

Warwick Charlton was on deck to greet us with a cigarette at 4 o'clock this morning. He had apparently been up all night. He seems to live on his nerves.

After scrubbing down and then stamping letters all morning (me) the 'Old Man' called me up to the quarterdeck and suggested that I go on day-work for a week, get really 'stuck into' the letters and see that 100,000 – the entire stamp collection on board – were stamped, franked and boxed before next Sunday. He also suggested a $20 bonus for the hands that accomplished the feat, giving me a free hand in choosing and setting the machine in motion. The thought of $20 has really livened people up and this afternoon and evening volunteers flooded the Post Office which

I have set up in the small space of deck under and around my hammock, the only space free of clutter. There was also considerable controversy at the tea table as to how many should get the bonus. It seems the entire crew will volunteer, especially in watch time, and Villiers mentioned to me that I should choose a team of six only. I shall broach him on the subject tomorrow.

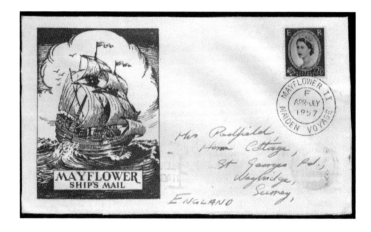

The wind came in fits and starts all day and this evening there were squalls and people started wearing brand new oil skins. It is positively the first rain since we left. Everyone is waiting for a bath. Maitland even stood around with his mouth open for a drink – so he said.

Reverting to the argument at tea. The trip is beginning to show people up now. One can't live in such close proximity to people for so long without learning a lot. I, personally, think I am very lucky to be on the ship at all. I didn't expect much in the way of accommodation, and I expected hard work, and a tough voyage. Admittedly the accommodation is pretty smelly, but the work isn't hard – especially with the three watch system, and as for the weather – it is ideal for a pleasure cruise. Yet there is dissatisfaction expressed by many – many who I should think were very pleased they were originally picked. They quote British Merchant Ship practice – overtime – etc etc. The

From left: Fred Edwards, Mait Edey, Mike Ford, David Thorpe, Graham Nunn.

chief culprit is Harry Sowerby, an old fellow whom I very much liked in the 'Digs' ashore, but who now appears to be the

complete grouser and sea lawyer with a strong distaste for work.[†]
Joe Lacey stirs up plenty of arguments but I think it is mostly his
Irish temperament and not particularly the context. Andy
Lindsay is just dying to get off the ship, which he can't call
enough bad names – but I like Andy. He does it in a very pleasant
way. The others are in good spirit, though.

Maitland Edey (top) and Joe Powell
playing chess.

Maitland has just beaten me twice at chess.

† In my youth I made no allowance for his age. He was a fine man.

Villiers and Ike Marsh, the Bosun.

LETTER III

15th May – 30th May

1957

Becalmed.

LETTER III

(For heaven's sake keep all
these letters very carefully.
They are my only diary of the trip)

Mayflower II
Mid-Atlantic,
Wednesday May 15th '57

Dear Mum,

Here beginneth the third epistle. As I write we appear to be shooting along once more although we have lain becalmed all day and most of yesterday with a glassy blue, mirror-like sea and plankton and little floating things visible a long way down. Every now and again a light breeze would spring up and we'd turn a complete circle. During this morning the 'Old Man' had the motor boat lowered overside with great danger to life and limb as it swung frantically on the derrick in this long Atlantic swell, and soon we were being towed at a steady knot to try and find some wind. Luckily we didn't find much and at noon practically all hands went for a dip in the beautiful blue, clear-as-crystal water. People were diving in from the fo'c'sle and the shrouds and having a great time – and, needless to add, the photographers had a field day. The Mate swam out to the motorboat – some 200 yards ahead – in full dress – trousers, shirt and woollen cap – with four bottles of beer for the crew. He looked like the 'Old Man of the Sea' appearing up the ladder dripping all over. Warwick Charlton was detailed for shark watch but half-way through he was found leaning nonchalantly against the Quarterdeck ladder. Ike, the Bosun, who can't swim, was towed along in a life buoy with frequent encouraging instructions from the deck to kick his legs – arms etc.

Wally went out for a swim rather too late, when a light breeze was pushing us along at a couple of knots. He got left behind at great speed, and even Graham, who dived in to help him, couldn't keep up. Luckily a handy heaving line was thrown from the poop and they were hauled aboard.

During the afternoon all hands, in relays, went out in the motorboat to take shots of the ship. She looked very impressive, even with furled and flapping sails and yards of film were rolled out from every angle. It is, of course, the first time we have seen her at sea – and it was really thrilling against the backdrop of fleecy white cumulus and the long, curved swell.

It has been really sticky and hot these last two days – like doldrum weather – not trade winds. Most of the time I have been below decks directing the Post Office, which is a going concern now, turning out between 12 and 18 thousand stamped, postmarked but unaddressed letters a day. The $20 bribe from the captain has worked wonders, as a dollar bribe always will, and enthusiasm is tremendous. I have everyone working two hours of their watch below and as much as they can in their watch on deck. There are three permanent day workers doing it, John Winslow, Graham Nunn and myself. Usually the gentlemen, Lee Israel, Julian and Warwick turn to in the mornings and do 'time and motion'

studies, but we are going to have a tremendous job to finish our quota by Sunday.

Washing clothes is the main problem, I find.

This evening all hands were called on deck at about 9 o'clock – just as I was packing up the Post Office – and we 'weared' ship for a moderate breeze that had sprung up from somewhere, and from the direction of the moon. I take it we are going in roughly the right direction with the yards braced hard up on the starboard tack.

The 1ˢᵗ Mate.

John Winslow in mid-Atlantic.

Coming up the ladder.

I shall be very glad to jump into my hammock tonight, as the overtime hours I have been putting in with the Post Office must be about four a day – together with heat, swimming and starchy food – all potatoes – chunks of bread, eggs and beans. The fresh food ran out some time ago. It is a very fleshy diet and I'm afraid I am beginning to show it amidships.

As an illustration of the efficiency of enthusiasm – during our spell of 'all hands on deck' this evening the Mate yelled "haul in the 'main tack'." I was standing by the main tack and yelled "Main tack – aye, aye, sir" and cast it off the port pins and started heaving on it grunting "hi-ho-hi-ho," in the approved fashion. In no time at all about fifteen people had tailed on to the end of it pulling for their lives, and the heftiest man aboard, Jumbo Goddard, was leaping up and down yelling in time as well. It was only after we had practically tacked the sail down that the 3rd Mate yelled "Wrong tack – starboard side" and we all looked suitably sheepish and let it out again.

Thursday 16th May

Gordon Tenney, from 'Life.'

We are still drifting helplessly at the mercy of wind and tide and tonight headed East into a beautiful gold sunset with the Mate turning the wheel idly and everyone shooting off Koda-chrome film. This morning wonderful cooling showers beat down from heaven and everyone except myself had a shower on deck. I didn't as I had had a fresh water wash previously and my tiny towel was soaked. Gordon was vainly trying to take photos for *Life* while most of the crew showering danced around in the nude 'ring-a-ring-a-roses' fash-ion.

Great strides were taken in the Post Office, one group on deck, one in the Great Cabin and one in the 'tween decks, everyone trying to make up for the time lost yesterday. Indeed, I drew 24,000 stamps and I estimate we stamped and franked 18,000 envelopes, which is just about up to schedule.

Still becalmed.

Some people seem to be getting bored with idling in the middle of the Atlantic – others seem to be quite happy in this really very pleasant climate. I don't have time to think about it. The routine of the ship never varies. Eight bells are struck, one watch musters on the port side at the back of the Quarterdeck, one on the starboard side. The Mate sees that all are present (only four in each watch during this so-called 'Trade Wind' spell). The lookout from the fo'c'sle yells "Lights are bright sir" (during the time between sunset and sunrise) and Maitland Edey's American drawl right on top of the bells every time is most expressive – and then the Mate says "Relieve the wheel and Lookout." Two figures stumble up to opposite ends of the ship, the man going up to the wheel taking care not to offend tradition by going up the weather ladder, and the relieved watch is then ordered below while the watch on deck settle themselves with a cup of cocoa at night or take over the previous jobs during the day. The jobs this week have been mostly with the Post Office.

And so it goes on. Today we had salt beef – very cheap stuff, mostly fat – and real 'hard tack', which will be something to talk about when we have to make up stories of incredible hardships. The conversations nowadays – when they are in any way serious – often hinge on the food that is going to be eaten when we get to the 'States'. Yesterday a French liner asked for our position and there was much speculation as to whether she would alter course to look for us; but she seems some way away now. We had decided upon all the things we would ask for if she appeared though – chiefest of which was ice-cream, closely followed by French girls.

Friday 17th May

Life will seem pointless without the Mail schedule to keep up. Today I drew 24,000 stamps from the 'Old Man' and I suppose we got through about 18,000. Everyone is pulling with a will. It is truly amazing what a little enthusiasm from a few groups of people will do. Everyone is very eager to put in his two hours overtime on the job and race each other. Beric claims about 1,600 letters stamped solo in one hour. Dave Thorpe seems to be about the best franker, keeping up a rhythmic tattoo with his stamp. Talk gets nearer to America and baths and linen sheets and milk shakes the longer we roll around in this long oily swell.

Again today we had variable airs and made little progress – a slight forward motion towards sunset perhaps. At noon we dived into the marvellously clear blue waters – no one strays far from the ship though – on account of possible monsters of the deep – sharks being favourite.

This morning an Italian emigrant liner, the Lusania, appeared from out of the blue and circled us once at full speed and very close before steaming rapidly away. Cameras clicked and a lot of people felt very frustrated at such close proximity with civilisation. There was a lot of cheering from both sides and cries of "*Viva L'Italia.*"

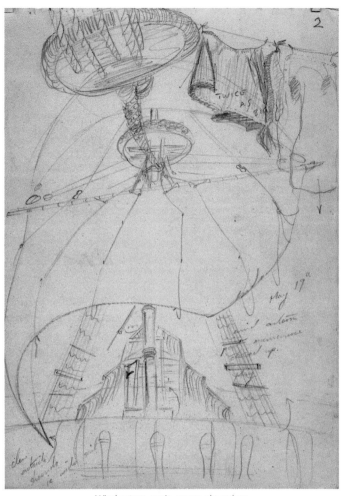

Wind astern, main course clewed up.

Saturday 18th May

Still floating along under a merciless sun. I drew the last 9,000 odd stamps from the 'Old Man' and at about 5.30 stowed the last envelope in the last box to the accompaniment of cheers of relief from the crowd (a term I don't generally like) who have been putting in a tremendous amount of enthusiastic overtime.

From top: Stuart Upham, 'Jumbo Goddard, 'Doc' Stevens.

The Old Man presented me with a bottle of whisky and two of rum for 'splicing the mainbrace' which I decided to do after dinner. Before dinner we had scattered heavy showers and Joe Powell and myself stripped off and soaped ourselves all over with the glorious fresh water. In the middle of it all I was told I was Peggy to shouts of laughter at my lathered condition. Joe Powell was caught in a similar condition some minutes later when the watch on deck squared yards. Joe rushed around heaving with the best, stark naked and white with soap. It was excruciatingly funny to watch him among the oilskinned figures on the Quarterdeck. After dinner I put on a bathing costume, frilly blouse which I found in a rag bag, bra and with a Postmistress sign around my arm helped Wally the cook to prepare and serve a fruit cup made with the rum. It was quite successful and we accompanied it with a sing-song and an attempted assault on Warwick Charlton, the organiser of the project, in which we tried to postmark his bare bottom. It proved unsuccessful though. Later I had a few rums in the builder's (Stuart Upham) cabin and so to hammock where, I was later told, I was the object of a procession of the afterguard who thought it extremely amusing that I should be lying flat on my back looking drunk. I wasn't – drunk I mean.

Sunday 20th May

We were all very relieved that the Church Service was not in fancy dress and we sat around, cool on the Quarterdeck as the 'Old Man' read the lesson, prayers and then gave us the usual breezy

Villiers talk. This week, instead of the Pilgrims of *Mayflower*, he talked of "that nut Columbus." He is a very amusing, bluff, studiedly sailorlike speaker but holds and interests his audience "--- Columbus was nutty when he started the voyage. I don't know where he lived – but if he lived up here (pointing to his cabin) I am not surprised he wasn't a lot more of a nut before the end of the voyage." (laughter).

Villiers on poop, looking for wind.

He talked of sailors "---not the emaciated, effete Westerners but real sailors such as the Arabs ..." He went on to describe some comments he had heard in an Arab dhow "… the Lord has been too kind to the Europeans in the matter of money and arms – but they have lost control of their women and they're going all to hell – quite right too" (laughter). Earlier he took some time to disprove the accepted ideas about Columbus being the first across to America, and said the Vikings had done it many times before by the Northern route "--- those tough guys didn't have maps. They were only interested in loot and women – tangible merchandise – quite right too" (looking round at the assembled company with his head poked slightly forward on his heavy shoulders and a broad grin on his face). These are a disconnected series of phrases that I remember among a lot of such typical stuff. He talked of Columbus because we are following in his tracks. He also mentioned that during the last week of light, variable airs we had made good 400 miles due mainly to the current. Today we seem to have been going along fairly steadily before a shifting wind mainly in the East. The 'O.M.' said that the ship's maximum speed was 7 knots[†] but she 'ghosted very well' which is very true – and she steers very well when ghosting. He prophesied roughly three weeks to the Nantucket light – or was it Plymouth harbour?

After the talk he wanted to check our passports and the Cook distributed cigarettes, chocolate and sweets. Mine always go the first day. I spent the rest of the day sketching or sleeping in the most ridiculously uncomfortable positions, draped across hatchboards or lying flat on wooden decks. I should have brought a chair on this trip as there are very few comfortable positions apart from the horizontal in bed, and the continual rolling does not help.

This week has been notable for glorious sunsets, as spectacular as any I can remember – blazes of gold turning to flame orange and red and tipping receding layers and layers and layers of jaggedly topped cumulus clouds in concentric parallels for hundreds of miles down to the horizon of bright, steel blue sea. There is a sing-song at the moment led by Beric Watson and his guitar.

Another remark by the 'O.M' this morning was when he was explaining the difficulty of someone not belonging to the aristocracy commanding one of the Spanish expeditions. He told us how Columbus always signed his name with an indecipherable cypher – "perhaps because he was ashamed of his plebeian upbringing – in that case he had no need to be."

[†] *But see Stuart Upham later suggesting she would be able to make more with bonnets and staysails rigged (p. 67).*

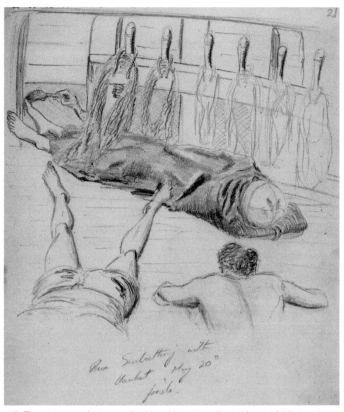

Different approaches to sunbathing. Note pin rail on side, to which running rigging is belayed and coiled.

Joe Powell and the night-callers. Joe Powell, the ex-commando man mountain who has been on the 12-4 watch for the last week, appears to be having hallucinations (or very bad dreams). He fumbled out of his cabin at 6.35 this morning as I was getting out of my hammock and asked me what time it was and why I thought he had been called. I assured him that to my knowledge he had not been called and he retired disbelieving and cursing sleepily. Later that morning I went down again and a plaintive voice called from his cubicle "What's the time – who's called me?" He can never remember who calls him, although he thought it was Dave the first time, but is quite certain that he is called at odd hours during the night and to make his assertions carry weight he says that he has already traced two series of previous callers. His intense seriousness about the whole thing is excruciatingly funny.

Warwick Charlton; left. Lee Israel relaxed on the boat cover.

Another man suffering from watch-keeping is Maitland Edey. In his own words "I asked the Mate a question about Gordonstoun school and that was the last thing I knew for 20 minutes. When I woke up he was gone." He had dropped right off to sleep on his feet in the middle of one of Godfrey Wicksteed's interminable absent-minded monologues.

Tuesday 21st May

We are moving again before an E'ly wind of about force 5. No one can understand why we are not moving faster – as fast as a force 5 used to send us. The 12-4 watch – after a week of long

sleeps – is doing us no good. It is damned hot during the day, and a bit too cool for comfort during the night. All in all I am listless. Starting to read 'Claudius the God'. Lee has been catching Sargasso weed which drifts past the ship in great quantities in a home-made fishing net. It is very interesting to watch the camouflaged crabs and tiny starfish which cling to the weed – and all sorts of miniature 'Quatermass' monsters.

Lee fishing for Sargasso weed from forward Starboard channel.

Wednesday 22nd May

Was chiefly notable for an excellent sing-song in the evening to celebrate Dick Brennan's birthday. The sun set splendidly and then a quarter moon looked down on the sea and the crew sitting to starboard of the lifeboat with a lantern shining up into the circle of faces. Incorrect – the moon rose during the 12-4 watch – but it was a balmy warm night – the sort that one signs on to go to sea for. The music from John Winslow, Beric Watson and 'Scotty' with his thimbles and pail was lively and the Mate sang some amusing verses and part of a 17th century song. We all retired suntanned and happy. During the party Wally, the cook, presented Dick with a birthday cake which he attempted to cut – but after scraping away layers of dough and paste, came to a very solid tin that had contained fruit. A rum punch was served with a lot of titbits, sausage rolls, biscuits etc.

During the day we thought the wind had returned as she had periods of flying along in her old style, but by midnight she had sobered down to the inevitable 2-3 knots again. While checking the sails some wind chutes were found and set up at the fore end of the hatch and into the galley. They might do something to relieve the stuffiness but a great many people sleep on deck now in the lifeboat cover.

Thursday 23rd May

Ghosting still to light airs. A bonnet – which is merely an extension to the sail – was set on the foresail this morning, more, I think to say that it had been done than to increase the speed – but it appears to be pulling her along faster. The stuns'l has also been reset but not the lateen as the 'Old Man' has built a tent-like structure over his cabin, which will probably restrict the lateen. I had quite a long chat with him this afternoon while at the wheel and told him of my visit to the Maldivian buggalow [a type of dhow] in Columbo. He remarked that he didn't know any of the 'whites' in Columbo because it didn't help him in his dealings with the Maldivians if they thought he was in the European circle. He seemed very surprised that I enjoyed our six week stay in Columbo. Another pleasant aimless day in which we oiled down the masts and all the wooden blocks. Things have come to the pitch in our watch when Fred whipped into the Bosun's chair from under my feet as I was oiling the pole atop the mizzen mast in order to find a job. Beric also offered to hand an oil can inboard for the same reason while Mait ambled around with an oil can, then without an oil can, and finally stood by a few ropes. There is not much to do on deck and one has a suspicion that some of the jobs are manufactured. Ike, the Bosun, complains that anyone would think she was going to be at sea for another three years – not three weeks. No one anticipated the trip being as long as looks to be – the 'Old Man' said to me today that had she been his Maldivian buggalow we would be making the Nantucket light by now with the winds we have had. He gave their maximum speed as 11 knots. The

The bonnet extending the fore course downwards. Beyond is the spritsail.

builder, Stuart Upham, was saying yesterday that it was nonsense that our maximum speed is 7½ knots. He seemed to think she would do a lot more with the bonnets set and the staysails – "she's got no canvas up at all." A lot of people, especially the Americans, Mait and Andy, seem to want to get the trip over quickly and with this feeling there seems to have come a cessation of talk about the food and drink at the other side -- although whether it is only temporary I don't know. I am still perfectly content with this ideal weather. This morning saw three porpoises swimming sedately abreast of the beak but they soon tired of the slow motion and disappeared. Lee still catches sargasso weed with an improved net, which is really a net. Fred Edwards' voice is still heard practically continuously through day and night. I am working up some of my sketches in pen and ink. Here are some of the verses of a 'Western Brothers'-style song done very well by John Winslow last night. It is, I think, the third song to be made up by the combination Watson and Winslow.

> Warwick is the man who thought of this show
> He organised everything, made it all go.
> What do we think chaps? We think it's a bloody good show
> This sailing again of the *Mayflower*.
>
> > Rather!

> Young Stuart Upham built this ship
> Built it to travel at a clip
> There's been an awful lot of lip
> About the speed of the *Mayflower*
>
> > Bad show – I'd say

> In 300 years England's done very little
> The population has begun to whittle
> People still go to the U.S.A. to settle
> But they don't go on the *Mayflower*.
>
> > It's not cricket

> The *Life* photographer is a bit of a lad
> His photographs aren't really so bad
> It's a pity the fellow's an absolute cad
> His folks didn't go on the *Mayflower*.
>
> > He's done his best!

> The world's full of descendants, so they say
> There seem to be a few in the old US.A.
> And in a short while I dare say
> There'll be a few more on the way.
> Sons of the *Mayflower*!
>
> > Stiff upper lip, old boy!

etc. etc. some not repeatable.

From left: Beric, 'Scotty', John Winslow.

Saturday 25th May

This is the day we were due in Plymouth, Mass. It started with the usual variable airs and gradually a swell built up from the N.E. where force 10 winds have been reported lately. Soon after lunch the 'Old Man' decided to go for a row in the pram to take pictures of the ship, which was, by now, becalmed. Beric Watson was detailed to row the little cockleshell around the ship once to prove her seaworthiness. He did so successfully and then the 'Old Man' risked life and limb, dignity and hundreds of pounds worth of cameras in trying to board her in the heavy swell. One minute she was 15 feet down below the gunwale, the next about level with us – but he finally clambered in and was pulled along looking – as before – like a contented Mr Toad huddled in the back. The whole thing looked very unsafe with not more than 3" or 4" freeboard aft. He returned to the ship and then Gordon and Lee went out to take photos – and bail frantically – while I was at the wheel. A light breeze blew up from the N.E. while the pram was a long way away and the 'O.M.' yelled out to them to return to the ship. The yards were then braced on the starboard tack and we were soon on our way again, with a wind ever slowly freshening. We are bounding along now – and moving around a lot in the swell.

'Scotty' and Beric bathing on deck.

This morning a rain shower disturbed the deck sleepers at about four o'clock and later another one brought forth naked bodies with bars of soap and back-scrubbing enthusiasm. I was just too late though and couldn't find a drop from the cumulusy sky. There is still a lot of sargasso weed floating past. The Mate determined our speed by log line at 4 o'clock as 5.4 knots. I think it is more now.

This morning some wonderfully luminous green dolphins glided gracefully abeam of the ship and resisted all attempts at hooking them. One big fellow chased the bait for some time but never snapped at it. They seldom broke the surface of the water but twisted and turned just under the surface making a very lovely picture of beauty in motion, and soft shades of colour. Whether they would be such subtle tones out of water I don't know. We never had a chance to find out as a rain squall came in from the North and drove away the fishers – drove them naked to the starboard side of the main deck to lather themselves with the luxury of fresh water soap – and a civilised smell.

Sunday 26 May

I have just come off look-out, which we now keep perched up on the fore yard. The bonnet on the foresail has obscured the sidelights which were always dim, being oil burning since it was found the electric installations were not up to M.O.T. specifications and it has also interrupted what little view the lookout used to have from the fo'c'sle. We are getting wise to the situation up there now and sit on a lifejacket on the parral which makes a comfortable enough perch for an hour. Mait Edy always lashes himself to a handy shroud as he says he 'keeps on dropping off' (to sleep). This morning I very nearly dropped off from shock. I was sitting up there singing a little ditty to myself when six bells went – a signal for the end of my spell aloft and also a signal for me to yell "Lights are bright, sir." For some reason no one this watch had called out the "Lights" business on time, and unbeknown to me the Mate was right behind me on the shrouds as the bells went. When I, too, forgot to call out "Lights are bright" he cut in just by my right ear "Did you hear six bells?" "Yes." "Well, why didn't you report the lights?" The shock of the voice from where no voice was expected was unpleasant.

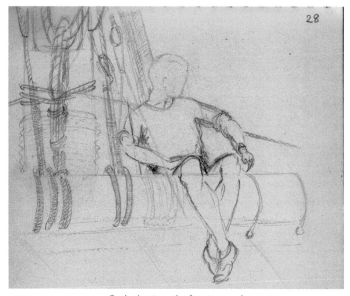

On lookout on the fore top yard.

I have been thinking back over a conversation last night in which Mait and Andy Lindsey in particular were discussing the difference in the attitude of the crew towards work now and when they first joined. Then it was "Yes, sir," "No, sir," "– Can I coil this rope – shall I polish the mast, sir?" All eagerness, enthusiasm and greenness. As Andy put it "A bunch of greenhorns – strictly wet behind the ears." Now most people are old hands – only work in their watch on deck and are not so terribly keen about that, making most good jobs spin out.

Andy and Harry Sowerby, who is always grumbling about something, seem to think the crew is being exploited – "working in the Dog watches – working on Saturday afternoon – Easter Bank Holiday Monday – loading ballast and treasure chests" etc. I said they knew they could do it because of the law of supply and demand – 3,000 people after 30 jobs on the *Mayflower*. Andy said that was no excuse for exploiting the boys. Earlier in the day Harry said "They've broken every rule in the book" (referring to crew employment).

Another quotable quote from Andy "I think England's strictly for the birds – but they do make good candies and good biscuits – yes sir!"

The fo'c'sle windchute with its flaps stretched to the shroud looks like Christ in a nightgown addressing the crowd with sweeping gestures. From just below on the starboard side it looks rather like the crucifixion. The sails at night are lovely shapes and take on different complexions according to the brightness of the moon. Tonight the sliver of moon was behind clouds but the sails seemed whiter than ever in the greater darkness – whiter and more puffily curved like the 'white owl sweeping'! The 2nd Mate has slung his newly-made hammock right across the after entrance to the 'tween decks and everyone coming up and congregating for the relief of the watch has to duck underneath. The bell is just above him and is struck every hour so I don't think his chances of uninterrupted sleep are very great.

11.00 We have just finished Church service in the bottom half of our fancy dress. Afterwards the 'O.M.' gave us another history lesson, starting from where he left off last week, after Columbus and taking us up to the British domination of the Atlantic after the defeat of the Armada. He referred to the dozen or so birds we have seen lately, advancing them as the reason Columbus thought he was near land and so headed S.W. with a migration of them. Had he not done so he would have been carried North by the Gulf Stream and probably never made land at all. Referring to the birds "– I don't know how they make a living. We are 1,000 miles away from the nearest land – the Windward Islands of the West Indies." He also said we have 1,700 miles to go and could do it in two weeks with reasonable luck. Other quotable quotes: discussing the difference between Pilgrim Fathers and Puritans "– the Pilgrim Fathers were fleeing from religious intolerance – the Puritans were intolerant of the English. They were a stiff-necked lot of bums that still hang around Boston today. You'll see them." All the non-whiskered members of the crew are having their portraits taken by the *Life* photographer now, which means I have to put on the TOP half of my fancy dress.

Defending the Anigoni portraits and the Royal Family as a symbol of the normal British family against Warwick Charlton on deck this afternoon, the 'O.M.' appeared from the saloon and, finding the topic under discussion, told Warwick that a dose of presidents would cure him. He then offered a bottle of rum for the first man at the wheel to find and hold the trade winds. I went up at 1 o'clock to take over the wheel from Fred, by which time a force 2 had sprung up. By quarter past, though, it was blowing a steady 4 from the N.E. We had been becalmed again during the morning.

Monday 27th May

Feeling much fitter after the first good night's sleep on the 8-12 watch. Scraping decks in the fo'c'sle part of the 'tween deck in the morning. In the afternoon the tanker *Belgian Pride* circled us with all halyards streaming with flags and dropped a parcel which the Doctor fetched in the pram. The parcel contained cigarettes, chocolate, eau-de-cologne and a bottle of champagne brandy, which was totted out to the crew. All hands thought it was a very fine gesture from the Belgians.

Later Warwick Charlton was seen blowing bubbles over the lee rail for some minutes. He is living on his nerves now that we are getting later and later and his receptions and parties and plans are dissolving in the mists of time.

Tuesday 28th May

Scraping the pitch and filth off the 'tween decks is current. A diversion after lunch when the French liner *Colombie* sailed straight for us and circled once. Tremendous enthusiasm aboard

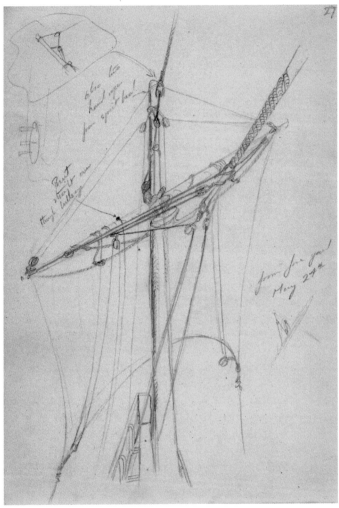

Beakhead, bowsprit, spritsail yard and sail.

and all the cameras were out in bloom. Later the first British ship, since the Brixham trawler the first night out, steamed up to have a look at us. She was the Royal Fleet Auxiliary, *Olna*, and she appeared to be having difficulty in catching us as we were flying along. Much regret was expressed aboard that we couldn't see ourselves as she was seeing us. She used every known method of signalling in typical Navy fashion, first with the lamp, to which we could not reply as ours is non-operative, then with semaphore and finally with flag. The morse said that she would do anything we wanted and that we looked as pretty as a picture; the flags were WAY, wishing us a pleasant voyage, and then 'God Speed' in plain language, and the semaphore was "You look just like an oil painting". We were about to send back "I bet you say that to all the girls" but were not in a favourable position for semaphore. Fred Edwards was in his element on the poop, waving his arms madly and pretending to read the message, which was actually done by Andy Lindsay. We gave her some rousing cheers as she closed to within about a cable and finally made off, streaming black smoke. As she came up the Mate was at some pains to see that our diesel generator was shut off in case they photographed the exhaust and the overflow.

I am sketching madly at every available opportunity to try and complete a series of the entire rigging. Also designing a camera case for Joe Powell's film business and trying to write brief notes to all my acquaintants in the *Mayflower* postmarked envelopes, of which I will be sending you some – without notes.

I must quote from a letter I am writing to Joanne, as I think this bit, written at about 4.45 a.m. after coming off watch, is rather good. "The thing which I expect to remember about this trip more than anything else is the shape of the sails. I have tried to capture them in sketches but they are strictly two-dimensional and rather pedestrian. The sails are winged" (unquote) and so to the 8-12.

Quotable quotes from earlier in the trip. 1st Mate – "There is no greater pleasure in life than pulling in the second turn of a rolling hitch. You don't need all those false pleasures you go after." (To Beric). On hearing the bells one day, "Good Lord! The right number of bells at the right time!"

Fred Edwards – on diving into a tin of jam – "One Board of Trade strawberry per ten cubic centimetres" – on the near approach of the French liner in his bumboat[1] accent, "Hey you, mister – what sorta beer you got dis ship?"

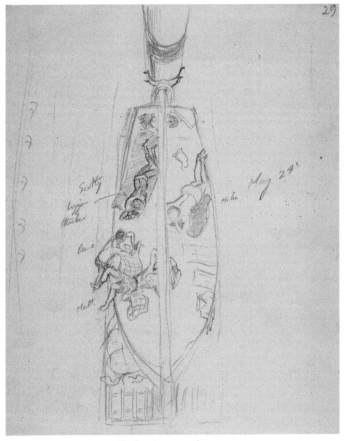

The boat cover as lounger.

[1] *A small boat used by port traders to convey supplies to ships moored offshore.*

Scraping the 'tween decks.

Wednesday 29th May

Scrape, scrape, scraping and sweating profusely in the 'tween decks. While sketching on the tiller flat table in the afternoon Maitland Edey said he'd take a selection of my drawings to *Life* magazine if I so wished. I said that would be a good idea and he intimated that they would pay well if they did publish any. In the evening I experimented with the cross-staff (the old fashioned method of taking angles of the sun) first theoretically with Jan Junker, the 3rd Mate, and then practically with the Mate and his sextant. We found that the large angles came in well enough if the end of the staff was thrust almost into the eye socket; but the smaller angles didn't come in at all.

There was a rhubarb session this morning apparently with most of the members of the Dog watch, Dave and Andy Lindsay discussing with Warwick why there should be any discrepancies in pay for equal work. Some people are getting A.B.'s rates of £32 a month and some 1/- a month. I think everyone concedes that the entire crew could, if necessary, have signed on at recognised rates just to get the job, but as some people are getting normal rates – the majority, in fact – why shouldn't everyone? My view is that the matter should have been brought up when we signed on, not now – but I kept quiet. They seem to think that they have Warwick Charlton on toast now if they did threaten any adverse publicity for the project.

In the evening we awaited the arrival of the R.F.A. tanker *Tidal Osprey* which showed up where expected at about 20.15. Maitland Edey sighted it on lookout, and thus earned himself a drink from me – as we had a bet on the first to report a light – neither of us having yet done so. She under-estimated our speed and came up with us from the port quarter while the Mate shone the searchlight on our sails. Everyone bemoaned the fact that we couldn't answer her morse without an aldis lamp but eventually she sent "Good luck, good voyage" and, at two blasts of the whistle we lit flares from four vantage points on the fo'c'sle, well deck, quarter deck and poop, and illuminated the ship very effectively. Warwick Charlton was dancing around saying "Isn't this great – eh – eh? Isn't this marvellous?" The photographers were having a field day and most of the crew seemed to be lining the well deck very excited as the rows of lights drew nearer. I was at the wheel. After the flares, she turned a searchlight upon us but turned it off when almost abeam and about one cable away, whereupon we lit three more flares and Warwick danced up and down with excitement again. Edgar Mugridge led three cheers and we heard them cheering from across the water.

Earlier in the evening I had been experimenting (sorry – I have already described that).

Thursday 30th May

Sweating like galley slaves in the heat and stench of the tiller flat after chippie had dismantled the table. We scraped all the planks during the 8-12 watch and then had a luxurious time trying to clean ourselves up afterwards. While still naked we had to duck around bracing the fore-yard. At one bell, the change of the watch (12.30) we all fell in naked, except for Beric Watson, who had not been dirty as he had been sharpening our scrapers the entire morning and peggying later. He dropped his shorts in sympathy with us and the 2nd Mate sent us below in mock

Scraping the 'tween decks.

horror. In the afternoon the Doctor performed a minor surgical operation on my back removing a small non-malignant growth. It was watched with interest and when he said "You might feel some cold water running down your back now." Fred piped up with "cold water be damned! That's blood – buckets of it." Shortly afterwards the French liner *Antilles* (Le Havre) appeared on the horizon from the port quarter, soon overhauled us and shot past at great speed with a fine spray coming up from her bow-wave. She looked a very impressive sight with all hands and the cook on deck lining the rails and the starboard gangway, and we were very disappointed that she did not circle us at all, but headed away to the S. W.

In the early hours of the morning – after coming off the 8-12 watch – Warwick Charlton was holding forth about his experiences with 'Monty' in the desert.[1] He obviously respects him greatly and talks very interestingly about him, especially his first meeting with the Staff Officers after relieving Auchinleck. They all went away from the meeting spreading the gospel to the divisional commanders that there was a 'nut' arrived as C. in C. who would not countenance British troops being taken prisoner at any cost. "There is no honour in being a P.O.W. The Japs have a higher sense of honour." Within a fortnight the very lax morale of the 8th Army became transformed.

A few random afterthoughts. The 'Old Man' doesn't want the ship pinched up to windward at all and frowns heavily on anyone using down helm. This morning when we were scraping the tiller flat there was no one at the wheel. She steered herself on a N.W.'ly course with the wind abeam. The Mate was working as hard as anyone, lying flat on his stomach to scrape under the benches and getting filthy and sweaty. This afternoon he turned up in his pilgrim trousers (thick and heavy) cap and frilly shirt – so whether that means that he has no change of clothes I don't know. Certainly I have only seen him with one pair of shorts, which hang low always exposing his underpants above them with the inevitable blue shirt tucked inside. He usually wears his pilgrim shoes too. This evening (12.30 a.m. actually) Beric, Mait

[1] *I was not aware at this time what a remarkable man Warwick was. During the war he had served as a very young officer on General Bernard Montgomery's staff in the north African desert campaign of the Eighth Army. He was credited with changing Montgomery's image with the troops from distant and austere fanatic to the approachable 'Monty' dressed in sweater and Tank Corps beret instead of peaked cap. Warwick edited The Eighth Army News and several other service newssheets in which he was never afraid of criticising Churchill's government. And it was during this period that he conceived the idea of strengthening Anglo-American relations by building a replica of the Pilgrim Fathers' Mayflower and sailing her across the Atlantic. All his considerable powers of imagination and persuasion were needed after the war to convert his idea into reality. Against the odds, he succeeded – as one result of which I was now enjoying a life-changing experience.*

and I had a bet on her mileage during the watch as she seemed to be clipping along. The Mate, on being asked, said the answer was sargasso weed, as the log had fouled it during the watch. He estimated 21 miles though and gave us a bottle of beer. Food is much freer nowadays – Huntley & Palmer biscuits in profusion – tinned mushrooms, kidneys etc – and I have been stuffing myself too full. Mait was given a bottle of whisky by the 'Old Man' and we are conspiring for a 'blowout'.

Jack Scarr showering!

LETTER IV

Mrs Padfield,
Home Cottage,
St Georges Rd.,
WEYBRIDGE,
ENGLAND   SURREY.

2nd June – 12th June

1957

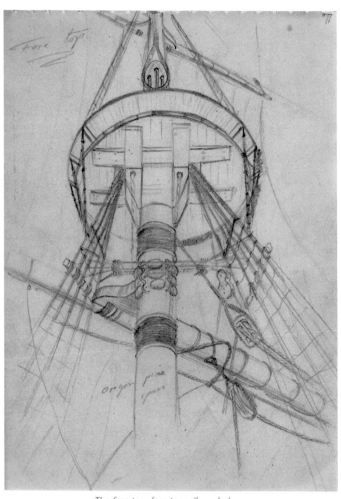

The fore top, fore topsail yard above.

84

LETTER IV

Sunday 2nd June

Heavy showers in the morning and some fresh water was collected in which I had a luxurious wash all over and felt a marvellous feeling of well-being. The wind has moved round to the East (force 4) which is just where we want it to be – that is just where the people who want to reach Plymouth want it to be – and we are bowling along well. The 'Old Man' held the customary Church Service at 10 o'clock but the imminence of showers discouraged his original intention of a crew photo in full fancy dress afterwards. It also discouraged his little history lesson, which was disappointing. He made an inspection of the 'tween decks afterwards and the Mate made some comments about the general chaos in the space around my hammock, but none of the stuff is mine – it is all chucked down through the hatch by people who intend to pick it up later. The 'Old Man' mentioned at Church that we had about 900 miles to go and were now in the horse latitudes. The wind which we now hold may or may not last. The last two days I have been very busy trying to finish my drawings of the rigging of the ship – especially since Mait Edey said he would show them to the *Life* editor – and during the watch our main task has been humping sacks of rotten – or some rotten – potatoes over the side. We have a tremendous superfluity. There was a brief hope yesterday that a U.S. Navy ship would find us and swop fresh steaks and food for some liquor which we pulled out of the Bond Room for the eventuality but she missed us.

In the afternoon we gave Joe Meany a mock graduation ceremony as today is graduation day for him at home. Andy Bell and myself dressed up in peaked caps, beards and lifejackets and stood guard over the Old Man's door with oars. The Old Man, Warwick Charlton and Stuart Upham came out from his cabin and standing to the starboard of the steering wheel, called for Joe Meany to step forward from the assembled company on the quarterdeck. He was presented with a large manuscript and clothed in a gown and mortarboard while the photographers made hay. Afterwards they grouped us for unending ship's company photographs. We changed to the 4-8 watch and got some new recruits for the watches, all the day workers being disbanded. We have Edgar Mugridge, the 'Chippie' and Joe Lacey – also Jack Scarr when he is not peeling potatoes. Fred Edwards, the 'Blue Funnel' 3rd Mate is doing the week as a watch-keeping 4th Mate with the Mate. He started very quickly to shout out "Four bells," "Who's on lookout?" and so on and handing down empty cups from the quarterdeck for his crew members to put away.

Sunset through the shrouds

In the evening our watch party came off at about 8.30 and proved a howling success – literally howling and I'm sure we must have kept a lot of the other watches awake as we were singing very lustily. Besides the original four members of the watch we have the newcomers and a whole lot of the 'afterguard' brought along because they could provide a bottle-a-piece. We had whisky, rum oatcakes, biscuits, tinned fruit juice and fruit which Mait Edey had swapped with Wally the cook for a bottle of rum, bottled chicken and tinned sausages. Among the afterguard everyone was there except Julian Lugrin and Lee Israel, who went back with the Doctor's watch last week.

Tuesday 4th June

Here I lie in the twilight in Lee's bed struck down by some wretched back trouble which – like your complaint – is impossible to diagnose. I got out of my hammock this morning and practically collapsed every time I put any weight on my right leg. I thought it was a touch of rheumatism or something similar, but it persisted after I had tried to use my legs climbing up the mast to go on look-out. When it came to washing down decks and lifting buckets movement became agonising so I went and lay below.

The doctor came to see me after breakfast and sent me to bed where I have been ever since intermittently trying to read 'Vintage Verse' and Evelyn Waugh's 'Black Mischief', and cursing my infernal luck. The day in bed doesn't appear to have done it any good as it was as bad as ever when I tried to walk up just now. Everyone has been very good indeed, the Doctor providing me with two tins of grapefruit juice, one of apricots and besides that some cake and chocolate of his own.

There has been great excitement today as three aeroplanes circled low overhead continually. All I could see from my bed beneath the hatch opening was a square of blue sky and the foot of the mainsail bonnet flying from one side to the other as the planes crossed. Warwick Charlton was apparently in ecstasies of enthusiasm again, leaping up and down and trying to flag the aircraft in with his handkerchiefs. Gordon, the *Life* photographer, packed up his photographs and captions in a waterproof case and lashed life jackets to it twice as rumours filtered down that one of them was about to land – but none of them did. Suddenly there was a shout "She's dropped something" and other voices took up the chorus "Something in the water – right ahead." "Launch the dinghy," "Maybe we can get it with a painter" and Beric Watson's voice above the rest endeavouring to get the dinghy overboard. Then the Captain's

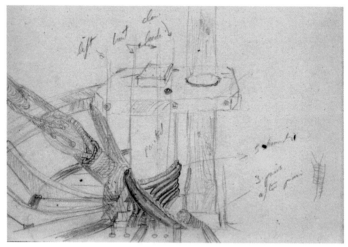

The topmast meeting the lower mast inside the top.

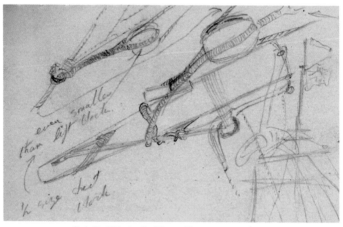

Detail of blocks for lifts and braces at yardarm.

stentorian growl "Back the main yard, Mr Mate"✝ and later "Ease the spritsail sheet." The ship appeared to take on a different motion; I could no longer see the mainsail flapping and voices speculated as to whether there might be mail in the floating object. John Winslow – "Shave a dog – wouldn't it be great to get a letter from my girlfriend." Joe Powell – "Well, if you don't get one from your girlfriend and I get one from my wife I'll read it to you." Eventually it turned out to be yesterday's copy of the *New York Times* and a couple of magazines – probably an impromptu gesture and all that they had in the plane. Tonight the 'hot scoop' is that a U.S. Navy destroyer will contact us early tomorrow morning – curse this back! Tonight I will try sleeping in a bed (Lee Israel's) for the first time since we left Plymouth while Lee sleeps in my hammock. What a way to end the voyage – for there is a feeling in the air that we are near the end now – with only about 750 miles to go and the ship still moving – albeit not so far as yesterday – to an Easterly wind.

Yesterday we clipped along (132 miles) with the wind just abaft the beam about force four and the yards almost square. As Villiers said "You get more power from the vessel with yards square." We cleaned the interior main deck paintwork down and today they started painting it – I believe. Yesterday when Ike Marsh, the Bosun, woke after the party at about four o'clock when we called his room mate Joe Lacey, he muttered apropos of nothing "N-A-R-L-S, Narls – a bloody fine woman" which we thought quite amusing – even at four o'clock – after a party. The Old Man made quite a memorable remark the other day when we were expecting a U.S. Navy destroyer en route to Reykjavik which had offered to provide us with anything we asked for, and it was suggested that the wind might freshen and so prevent us lowering a boat. "I hope so – I'd rather have progress than ice-cream."

✝ *Thus bringing the wind on the forward side of the mainsail and taking the way off the ship.*

The author sketching the rigging.

Wednesday 5th June

This is most frustrating. Tremendous excitement at 5.30 a.m. this morning when two Italian destroyers swooped alongside. All hands were called on deck – I lay in this wretched bed listening to the babel. The 'Old Man' growled "Hard up the mainsail Mr Mate." Someone shouted "Put the pilot ladder over." Voices contested loudly as to whether they should "Let go" or "Hold on" to something and eventually a boarding party of Italians came aboard with a jug of vino and a box of something or other. Above me voices, "What a marvellous sight," "Isn't this wonderful – eh – eh?" (Charlton). "What fun." "You think you're going to get any breakfast do you?" (Dick Brennan – assistant cook). Then "Trim the Mainsail, Mr Mate." But it wasn't long before another four destroyers were sighted and another boarding party came aboard. "*Viva l'Italia* – *Viva l'Italia*" – "*buona fortuna*" – "Bravo – bravo – bravo", and every now and again "Three cheers, boys – hip hip – ". *San Giorgio, San Mario* were the names of the first two destroyers, so John Winslow says. We now await the arrival of the big American destroyers. The first thing the Italian officer said upon boarding was "Magnifico – magnifico" and flung his arms wide in a typically Gallic gesture.

The Doctor called me up on deck as the American destroyers approached and I took a few shots of the Yanks lowering a boat out and coming across and Mait and Gordon going back to their ship with all the *Life* photographs and so on.

Mait cannot fathom Warwick Charlton at all. He has been very suspicious of him during the latter part of the trip, thinking that Warwick was going to send the Project's pictures off before *Life*'s and not being able to pin him down to a definite 'no' on the subject. Now, however, the *Life* photographers are aboard *U.S.N. Ault* steaming for Bermuda and Charlton's photographs are still aboard. He is apparently very annoyed with Lowe,[†] his partner, not making a rendezvous with us before now.

Quite an amusing incident just now by my bed as Jumbo Goddard, Edey and Gordon Tenney and the Doctor were pulling Lowe to pieces, saying "if he's a veteran car enthusiast, I'm a ---. If he ever handled a spanner he'd pull the pips off the nipple – " etc. (Jumbo Goddard is a veteran enthusiast) and "Dick says he's a Judo expert – must be from someone who couldn't do it either and found himself flat on the deck – ". When along came Charlton to see the Doctor about his bad leg which he knocked the other day, and started giving the lie to all three derogatory statements. Lowe is apparently a Judo black belt, a veteran car man, he does all his own repairs, a handy man with his hands (corroborated by 'Chippie' who appeared from the lower hold – "He could take away anything with those hands of his") and a double first from Cambridge with a great flair for speaking Russian. Jumbo's face was a picture while Warwick was expounding this. To return to the destroyers –

Mait and Gordon returned, the 'Old Man' sent them a present of salt horse (stringy, inedible, barrelled pork) to the wide grin of the entire company. The presents exchanged this morning were vino and messages from the Italian to us, rum in exchange from

---

[†] *John Lowe, Warwick Charlton's principal collaborator at this stage.*

91

us: then oranges, apples and carrots from the U.S. navy to us and whisky and some of the Italian vino in return – followed by the 'salt pork' as a final gesture. Afterwards the three other American destroyers teamed up on our starboard quarter in close formation, all the crew lined alongside, looking like rows of white ninepins. They were not really so close as the Italians who, according to report, nearly shaved our bowsprit off and also gave us alternate cheers from each ship, one on either side. I hope this makes sense. I am just writing it as it comes, trying not to leave anything out – no literary effort at all.

Jan Junker, 3rd Mate, came down yesterday, saw me lying in bed, hors de combat, saw Chippie sawing wood with a view to constructing a breakwater abaft the hausepipes to prevent the flood that struck us between Brixham and Plymouth if we are towed into Plymouth, Mass and said "What you make Chippie? a coffin?" which was very appropriate. He has a very dry sense of humour despite his habitually sad expression. His first famous

 remark (while still at Brixham) was "in bad weather – always eat apricots – they taste the same coming up or going down" and, after someone had tied a certain knot "Yes, that's all right – but sailors generally do it like this." Devastating. Yesterday he made a miniature lifejacket for Felix, the cat. Perhaps I haven't mentioned him yet. He was given to the ship in Plymouth by some old lady – I believe – and couldn't have been more than three weeks old – tiny. He has been looked after by Graham Nunn, the English cabin boy and is now a fierce, sailorlike animal with a strong nip and an inclination to scratch people unawares. The photographers have fun with him, putting him up ropes and snapping him coming down paw over paw.

We are now West of Bermuda – about 700 miles to go – and the popular idea is that we make it on Monday or Tuesday – Curse – Curse – Curse – Curse – Curse – Curse – Curse – Curse this leg.

Thursday 6th June

Clipping along at a great rate. A violent squall hit us at about 11 o'clock and all hands rushed around in oilskins – or nothing at all – taking in the topsails. There was a lot of shouting from on top and then the foghorn blew one blast at intervals, from which one would have supposed we were on the starboard tack. I believe we were on the port tack though. The hatch has been covered up because of the rain and I lie or sit here in the gloaming getting more and more fed up. The back does not seem to be quite so bad now.

Later – the back is, unfortunately, no better. This afternoon the main bonnet was taken in with great difficulty – I hear – because the cringles were too small for the lacing which had swollen during the rain. This morning there was considerable difficulty in getting both topyards down. The leather washer on the main topyard caught over some rope or other and eventually had to be marlin spiked off the parral. Everyone was very bucked with their own particular feats of derring-do.

Friday 7th June

We are still heading in the right direction with a favourable wind, and must be within 200 miles of Nantucket now. We are fairly clipping along and the topsails have been set again although the fore top-mast is leaning over at a crazy angle. At about 11.30 a *Daring* Class destroyer approached us signalling good wishes and another *Daring* and the *Ark Royal* steamed towards us from the horizon. The destroyer steamed slowly around us while Fred Edwards and Scotty Bell had some good signalling practice. She looked a fine sight with all hands cheering and waving, and I hope I got some good movies of her. Some minutes later the huge – comparatively – *Ark Royal* steamed along our weather side about half a cable away with, again, all hands lining the side and the forward ones peeling off and running aft as she passed. She carries about 1800 men and I estimate they were all on deck yelling and waving, and we must have looked a good sight as we were flying along with all sails full until she passed. Then our courses started flapping and the Mate flew into a fine rage (almost the first time I have seen him ill-tempered this trip). "Call themselves sailors!" he muttered. "Taking our wind – ". He directed his remarks at John Winslow, our Fleet Air Arm representative, who seemed taken aback by the onslaught. John had by this time rigged himself in his reefer jacket with sub lieutenant's stripes and wings, and white topped cap and binoculars and was dashing around more enthusiastically than anyone. His squadron were aboard the *Ark* and when she passed his voice could be heard above the general roar. "Stephen (or some such name) – hullo Stephen –" etc. During all this we were circled continually by two hovering helicopters, and when the carrier had gone past one of the two *Darings* steamed up our weather side kicking up a fine spray and a photogenic wash. That shot should be the best if it comes out on my cine. The Naval display continued for about quarter of an hour until noon causing great excitement aboard and bringing out cameras in full blossom. This was our first visit by the British Navy.

A Daring class destroyer approached us.

I went on watch for the first time since Monday to try out my back on light duties and the wheel. I felt perfect – and really think that it was only a pulled muscle – after all the Cheerful Charlies had been talking gaily of sacroiliacs – slipped discs – osteopaths etc. I drew until about midnight and then tried my hammock again. Julian Lugrin, the photographer, approached me almost sideways today about my sketches. He said they would have a tremendous market value in the 'States' having been done by a sailor aboard *Mayflower* as she crossed. He offered to introduce me to a friend of his in New York. "– if he had time." He said I should get between 1,000 and 1,500 dollars for the set. Julian is a clever chap, I think, and during the trip has always proved himself very helpful – and I am quite prepared to believe he is trying to do me a good tum. When I started the sketches I had no idea of the interest they would arouse – I don't even think they're terribly good – no style – although there are a couple of billowing sails that I do like.

Saturday 8th June

Anyway – back to the hammock – and a sore back. I am convinced the hammock has a lot to do with my back, now, as I woke with the same sort of strained pain this morning. However, it wore off as I took the wheel for the 5-6 spell and seems all right again now. During the watch the wind veered from about N.W. to just East of North, and at first we were making N.E. × E. At 7.00 a.m. we could only make E × ½N, and so weared ship and managed to make W.N.W. The 4-8 watch plus Ike and a few odd 'gentlemen' 'wore' ship and it went very well. I was at the wheel because of the back about which everyone is being very sympathetic, although I think it's going to be all right now.

At the moment we await an appointment with a U.S.N. dirigible.

I lost this pad for a couple of days and was really quite worried about it. However, here followeth a copy of a few notes I made on some scrap paper. The wind veered all Saturday and rose to force 7 in one afternoon watch, by which time we were rolling and pitching with enormous verve. She was taking the odd sea over green and we battened the hatch down and rigged up lifelines. I went on the wheel at 7 p.m. and it was not long afterwards that the 'Old Man' decided to 'heave to', called all hands on deck with three peeps on the 2nd Mate's whistle and then told his Officers off for the jobs; the Mate to the spritsail yard, the 2nd and 3rd Mates to the weather and lee sides of the mainsail respectively. When all hands were ready he gave the order "Furl the main and spritsail" and the clewlines and then the martinets and buntlines were heaved in with a will. However the spritsail then began to flap about wildly, shaking the bowsprit far more than it had when set, as the two clewlines and two buntlines are obviously not sufficient to brail up such a large sail area. The 'Old Man' got very agitated on the quarterdeck, repeatedly yelling to the Mate, asking him when he was going to get the 'bloody' spritsail furled and sending messengers to the same effect. He also told me to put the wheel over and run her off the wind – right down to S. W. – on a couple of occasions. During most of the evolutions I was steering W.N.W. with the wind just on the starboard beam. The Mate wanted to take the spritsail yard down to the beak to furl the sail but before he could do so Joe Lacey, our Irish monkey and prize rigging man, was out on the yard passing the lee gasket and Andy Lindsay went out with another length of rope to pass around the middle of the sail. They were followed by Beric Watson and the 2nd Mate and the four of them soon had the sail under control, although the yard was swooping up and down almost meeting the water at times like some fairground thrill-making machine.[✝] While all this was going on the boys from the mainyard were hauling up the foresail and then passing the odd gasket around it, while Mike Ford and Scotty went up to pass the gasket on the mainsail. When everything was furled (the lateen had come in some time before) and we were riding under bare poles the 'Old Man' ordered me to put the helm hard down or, in other words, with the wind on the starboard beam – 'hard a-starboard'. This was to test the theory that when these sort of ships were sailed in the 16th and 17th century they

[✝] *The most spontaneously brave action by these four that I have ever seen. Anyone who had fallen would have been lost under the hull.*

always hove to in this fashion. After some minutes with the wheel hard over and the vessel appearing to lie very easily with the wind

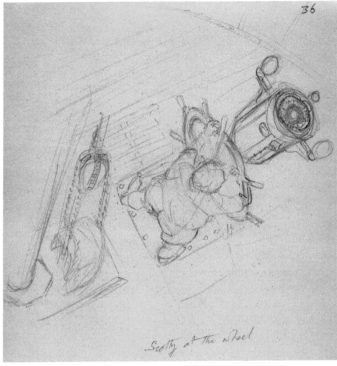

Scotty at the wheel

just for'd of the starboard beam I was ordered to lash the wheel in this position. She lay hove to with the wheel lashed all night – the high stern presenting a pushing surface to the wind which kept the bluff fore shoulder up into the sea – and there she stayed. Practical proof of the old idea. Possibly the rounded shape of the high stern had a certain aerodynamic form which might have given the vessel a little headway – I don't know. Anyway, she lay quite comfortably as the wind howled up to gale force 8, and heavy rain squalls beat down. As luck would have it I lost my oilskin jacket last Tuesday. The 'Old Man' re-enacted another centuries-old custom after the 'heave to' evolution, splicing the mainbrace on the quarterdeck and handing us each a generous tot of rum from an 'Old Navy Rum' bottle with his own fair hand – one by one. The photographers had a busy time with still pictures. Unfortunately it was too late for colour – as it was a very picturesque scene – the yellows, blacks and olive greens of oilskins set against the shining wood decks, and the brown and buff upperworks, the whole scene in constant motion with the sombre, white-flecked sea. I thoroughly enjoyed it on the wheel. She had been pitching and darting like a live thing.

Looking down on the quarterdeck, wheel and binnacle.

Sunday 9th June

I was on look-out from 4-5 a.m. and at 5 a.m. we set the foresail again and then the lateen, setting course N × W with the wind about E.N.E. or E × N. At the change of watch the two watches set the main and spritsails again – and we were on our way. After a short Church service at 10 a.m. the 'Old Man' remarked that we had only 130 miles to go and should be there some time tomorrow, using his favourite expression for these occasions – "if the Lord is good to us." During the day we were mentioned four times in an hour on the American News and, due to the time lag, were still apparently, 'hove to' in a gale. I'm glad we have had this gale. The 'Old Man' said he only 'hove to' to test out the ancient theory of riding with the helm lashed but it was lucky he did so as it became very necessary during the night.

Yesterday I had an interesting talk with Jan Junker, the 3rd Mate. We were watching the bowsprit weave and heave up and down like a whipping cane as the ship rolled and pitched, sometimes disappearing behind the foresail. Jan said that this gusty, squally weather would have been an everyday occurrence on the northern route and that we would have been very lucky to have any masts left in her by now. The inherent weakness of this early-type rigging is that there is no bobstay on the bowsprit to hold it down. Consequently when the fore-topmast stay is tightened it merely bends the sprit upwards. This means that it is impossible to tighten the topmast shrouds either. This accounts for the crazy angles the topmast has been taking up lately. Once the bowsprit or topmast came down in heavy weather it would start off a chain reaction, as the fore stay leads to the sprit and the main topmast stay leads to the fore top – and so on – a floating hulk. This essential weakness in the rigging seems to be the main reason the 'Old Man' chose to go South. The hull is as solid as it can be – despite complaints every day that someone's cabin is being flooded or bunk leaked upon – or that Jumbo can see the 'Southern Cross' through the side of the ship.

Monday 10th June

I have been sleeping in bunks ever since that last experience with the hammock. I went on deck at about 9 a.m. this morning to find us becalmed under a hot sun – although the water temperature has dropped to 68°. So much for our optimism. A U.S.N. submarine – heralded by our knowledgeable veterans as the *Nautilus* when it was still on the horizon – steamed quite close up and proved to be a bit of a tin can. The 'Old Man' bellowed "How's about a tow" and a semaphoring exercise started. I couldn't read it – mainly because it was too fast – also because I was busy letting go tacks and sheets and pulling on various lines as a 'volunteer' while we tried to put about on the port tack for a slight breeze that had blown up. Now we are heading South – straight for Bermuda again – albeit very slowly.

The submarine has disappeared – although rumour had it that she had agreed to tow us. Warwick Charlton was all for it, although the rest of the ship was buzzing with discontent – the ignominy – after 5,000 miles of sailing – of being towed in by – a submarine! The 'Old Man' was quite serious though, and had all our towing gear ready – he doesn't like our Westerly drift.

In the pram, Mike Ford bailing, Gordon Tenney rowing.

We have been making a little progress in the right direction since about 12.20 p.m. when we tacked ship onto the starboard tack for variable breezes between 1 and 2 mainly from the S.E. We have been managing to make good about N.E. x N, instead of the N.E. required, and are, according to the American wireless 60 odd miles S.S.W. of the Nantucket light. It has been a very warm, pleasant day and very eventful. We have been continually buzzed by aircraft of every description and velocity, including one huge six-jet bomber, reported the largest in the world. Various commercial craft winged around, and one yellow painted plane dropped packages in line to windward of us. As the wind was almost negligible the Old Man backed the main yard and Adrian Small went out in the pram to collect them. He was a long time away and a little striped figure in the boat, baling sometimes, picking up the floating packages one by one. The Old Man got impatient and called him back and also sent John Winslow swimming for a nearby one. They proved to be all beer – Hammonds – very nice and cold – but "just another commercial" (The O.M.).

More rumours of a tug throughout the afternoon and Warwick Charlton seemed put out about the antipathy shown by the crew to any idea of being towed to Nantucket – in fact the O.M. went around sounding out the crew on the subject this evening. Jan Junker is reported to have said "Yes – they don't want a tow now, all these tough sailormen – but give them three days becalmed !"

In the evening a fisherman came alongside and, after one unsuccessful try, we heaved a net of gigantic lobsters aboard, the biggest anyone had seen, one of whose claws was reported to be 7" wide. We sent him 400 Players and a bottle of rum on this third time round – for which they seemed very grateful.

There was a very touching ceremony after supper at 6.00 p.m. when the entire 'tween decks toasted Maitland Edey, the only gentleman who has worked in a watch the entire trip, and then admitted him into the fellowship of mariners, deep sea and foreign going, presenting him with a very professionally illuminated manuscript, scripted on vellum.[⚓] He was quite touched, as were a lot of the crew, especially, probably those who had been on watch with him; as he is an exceedingly fine man, deeply humorous, with a pleasant spaniel expression if caught doing something wrong, and a pleasing almost shy grin. He is a Princeton man, and can talk very interestingly on most subjects. The Doctor and Scotty initiated the ceremony and carried out most of the hard work connected with the production of the vellum and the seals. Fred Edwards once described Mait's eyes very pithily as the most chicken-stealing eyes he had ever seen.

[⚓] *Where did the vellum come from? My best guess at this distance in time is from the huge trunk Andrew Anderson-Bell (Scotty) carried with him to America – where he intended to find a wife and put down roots.*

Tuesday 11th June

This looks like the final day. After ghosting along all night we picked up a freshening breeze this morning and are now making about 4 or 5 knots with a Force 4 breeze on the starboard quarter. Today we have seen just about everything, and as the Doc said, "All we need now is a couple of Apaches on water skis and my day will be complete." Excuse the pencil but my ink spilled all over the deck in the rolling the other day.

We were roused this morning at about 5.45 to see the *Queen Elizabeth* steam past very slowly, looking very regal and blowing full blast on her sirens. There were not many passengers visible – probably behind screens. At the same time a tall sailing ship, which later proved to be the *Eagle*, could be seen on the port quarter making up towards us. Shortly afterwards a small slick-looking launch with nattily-yachting-suited characters and cameras and microphones sticking out everywhere came buzzing round us – all the people aboard shouting, grinning and yelling at once. I asked Mait if these were really, genuine Yanks, and he replied dryly that such people did float around in the States.

Hailing passing ships.

One of them proved to be Joe Meany's father (J.M. the American cabin boy). The next thing to appear was a coastguard cutter which signalled that she was escorting us to Nantucket. The *Eagle*, which is the American coastguard training ship, drew up on us very slowly which made Stuart Upham, our builder, wild with joy at the thought that the *Mayflower* could hold her. She was a lovely sight with the sun on her high sails and at about 9.30 she closed us to windward, exchanged ribald greetings with Villiers (the ribaldry came from Villiers) and gave us our course and distance to the Nantucket light – apparently 16 miles. All hands were on deck to cheer her – a thing which is unheard of for Americans apparently. During this time jets had been streaking and rolling past in their – by now – accustomed manner, and in John Winslow's ever repeated phrase "Cutting in their after-burners" – whatever that means. As the *Eagle* drew abeam the U.S. Navy dirigible (or blimp) sailed gracefully overhead. She is an incredible sight, occupying a huge area of the sky like a massive barrage balloon with four tails and bumps of radar and so on sticking out underneath. She blundered overhead like some prehistoric monster and gave the boys marvellous snaps by flying right over the barque *Eagle*. Shortly after this time a tug came in sight to escort us to Provincetown – escort, luckily. I'm sure that if we were becalmed she would be towing us.

One of the most amusing things this morning was the sight of Warwick Charlton dancing round and round the deck as the *Queen E.* passed and saying to everyone "Isn't it marvellous – eh? what a lovely sight!" Jumbo expected him to turn to jelly any minute. I expected him to evolve wings and take off. So – with everyone hopping around greatly excited, we sail in fine style towards Nantucket.

Noon. Nantucket light abeam, and around with the wind on the port quarter, to head N.E. ½N at a fine lick. Still circled by aircraft and closed by our escorting tug taking pictures – but work went on more normally than this morning, when none at all was started. I am trying to get all the Mail in by this evening to send ashore tomorrow – as it looks as if we will be there in the early hours. In the evening as arranged a birthday party for the Mate, which went off very well – lusty singing – plenty of gin, whisky and beer – and paté de foie gras (provided by Mait) – oh! and a vicious cup of pineapple and neat gin! At the same time Scotty Bell presented the 'Old Man' with a loving cup of silver, given by one of the members of the Royal Forth Yacht Club and we all drank Dimple Haig from it – and more Dimple Haig later. Scotty made a small speech about the very happy ship the 'Old Man' had produced and Villiers replied "– I thought I had a good crew – and I blooming soon knew I had –". He went on to say that we would be making a short stop at Princetown tomorrow, and that we were all to be on our best behaviour – and serious – "cause they're nice guys."

Wednesday 12th June

Probably the last time I shall be able to write up this letter regularly as we are at the moment being towed up the last stretch to Provincetown – and we are all rigging ourselves in 'fancy dress'. This morning I showed Maitland Edey my few drawings that I have done – and he seemed to think they were very good and said he would put them in his suitcase and take them up to *Life*. I hope something comes of it.

Mait Edey waiting for launch from a U.S. Navy destroyer.

I awoke at 12 this morning (midnight) with a splitting head (too much Dimple Haig and Grants Standfast) but it was soon blown away by an icy wind. The watch reached an all time low of only three mariners and I was the only one to report "watch is aft" at 4 o'clock. Beric being at the lookout and Joe at the wheel. This is because Mait has been knocked off watches for the last day, while Fred paces the quarterdeck as 4th Mate. We steer N.N.W. all the watch, trying to make more westing but the wind was about W × S, so we couldn't quite make directly for Cape Cod, which was sighted (the light) at about 01.15. We brailed up the topsail at 01.00 and set it again with the oncoming watch at 04.00. After about one and a half hours' sleep it was "All hands on deck" once more to furl all the sails and take the tug's towline for the final beat around Cape Cod against the wind – which we are now making. We used our anchor cable and the tug's rope hawser and shackled up after only one unsuccessful attempt with a heaving line which parted. Previously I had helped to furl the spritsail and afterwards I helped with the mainsail.

All hands are pretty excited now, although rain seems to be coming to damp our enthusiasm – and our pilgrim dress; and so far there are not many boats – no doubt there will be more shortly.

Last night the 'Old Man' questioned me about how much leave I had from P & O and I told him that I had as much as I wanted, and hadn't made any plans yet, whereupon he said that the Project might have to send a lot of people home from New York; which doesn't seem too hopeful for my chances of working by her for a time. Some people have already been asked to stay on – mainly the experienced sailors and our Canadian shipwright.

I hope you get all these letters soon. I shall close and post this as soon as possible – and hoping to receive a lot myself in a few hours' time. My plans – as I told Villiers at the wheel last night – are not formed at all. I shall certainly stay on in New York for a bit if asked to do so – otherwise fly home – I suppose. I hope these letters haven't been too technical and unreadable. I have done them partly as a record of the voyage – so please keep them safely – and also any newspaper cuttings. Also they have usually been done in great haste, on a table shaking with the diesel generator immediately below and tilting with the unpredictable rolling of the ship. Seldom has there been any silence – only loud talk and laughter and frequent interruptions. Further, I have been doing a great deal of work on my sketches – I hope with some rewards.

I expect I shall see you very soon and hear from you even sooner. I might or might not get a chance to describe our festivities in Plymouth.

I leave you with the 1st Mate's favourite heaving song.

"Yo-oh-ho – Ro-oll-ho,
For she drinks rum and chews terbaccer"

and lots of love

Peter

P.S. This has been a marvellous trip so far. I hope it stays that way in Plymouth.

The crew at Brixham.

Top row, from left: Edey, Horrocks, Charlton, Winslow;
Second row from top: Godfrey, Brennan, Goddard;
Clinging to shrouds, from top: Nunn, Lacey, Watson;
Row behind wheel, from left: Wicksteed, Church, Powell, Scarr, Marsh, Cauvin, Anderson-Bell, Edwards, Sowerby, Junker (behind Villiers's left shoulder), Mugridge, 'Doc' Stevens;
Level with wheel, seated left: Ford; standing: Small, Villiers;
Seated on deck front: Upham, Padfield, Thorpe, Meany, Lindsay.

Lateen and mizzen shrouds at sunset.

GLOSSARY

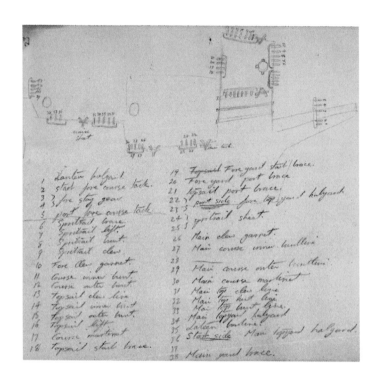

1 Lantern halyard.
2 start fore course tack.
3 } fore stay gear
4 }
5 } port fore course tack
6 } Spritsail brace
7 Spritsail lift.
8 spritsail bunt.
9 Spritsail clew.
10 Fore clew garnet.
11 course inner bunt
12 course outer bunt.
13 Topsail clew line
14 Topsail inner bunt
15 Topsail outer bunt.
16 Topsail lift.
17 course martinet
18 Topsail stud brace.

19 Topsail Fore yard start / brace.
20 Fore yard } port brace
21 Topsail port brace.
22 } port side fore top yard halyard.
23 }
24 } spritsail sheet.
25 }
26 Main clew garnet.
27 Main course inner buntline
28
29 Main course outer buntline.
30 Main course martinet
31 Main top clew line
32 Main top bunt line.
33 Main top bunt line.
34 Main topyard halyard
35 Lateen bowline
36 Start side Main topyard halyard.
37
38 Main yard brace.

110

GLOSSARY

Aback	when a sail is caught by the wind on the forward side
Abaft	behind, astern of
Abeam	positioned off the midlength of a ship
Aft	the back or stern of a ship
Back	(wind) to change direction anticlockwise
Baggywrinkle	rope yarns worked into anti-chafing gear
Beakhead	structure protruding from stem to hold bowsprit
Bobstay	line running from bowsprit down to stem to hold down the bowsprit (absent at *Mayflower*'s date)
Bonnet	supplementary canvas to increase sail area in light winds (later, the adoption of reef points allowed sail area to be reduced in high winds rather than expanded in light winds)
Bow	front of a ship
Bowlines	lines to edges of square sails to pull leading edge forward to attack wind at proper angle
Bowsprit	short mast projecting forward from stem
Brails	lines to haul lateen to its yard
Buntlines	lines to haul the foot of a sail to its yard
Cable	one tenth of a nautical mile, approximately 200 yards
Capstan	manually operated drum to haul in cable
Channel	horizontal timber projecting from ship's side to anchor and spread lower ends of shrouds
Clew	lower corner of a sail

Clewlines	used to haul the lower corners of sails up
Close-hauled	sailing with yards braced forward to maximum to steer as close as possible into the wind
Course	the lowest (and largest) square sail on a mast
Cringles	eyes sewn in to the boltrope running around the outer edges of sail to reinforce the canvas
Fo'c'sle	forecastle, raised deck at bow
Fore and aft	in line with ship's keel
Freeboard	distance between waterline and top of the side of a ship or boat
'Full and bye!'	to steer by the wind keeping the sails full without allowing the wind to catch the sails aback
Furl	to haul sails up to their yard using buntlines, martnets, clewlines, brails, finally securing the canvas to the yard by passing lines (gaskets) around the canvas
Futtocks	shrouds leading from the outside edge of the top down to the shrouds, fitted with ratlines so allowing the crew to swing up into the top
Gaskets	lines to secure furled sails to their yard
Helm	timber bar fixed through rudder head to angle the rudder; 'Helm up!' means moving the helm towards the windward, therefore high side of ship; 'Helm down!' means moving the helm to lee side
Jibboom	spar extending forward from bowsprit
Lateen	triangular sail set in fore and aft direction, in the case of *Mayflower II* from the third (mizzen) mast
Lee	opposite side or direction to that from which wind is blowing

Lifts	attached to ends of yards to adjust angle of yard to the horizontal
Martnets (or martinets)	lines to haul in the sides of the square sails
Mizzen	the third, and in *Mayflower II* after mast
Parral (or parrel)	assembly of timber rollers securing a yard to its mast, allowing horizontal angling
Pinched	the sails pointed very close into the wind
Poop	high deck at the stern
Port	left hand side of a ship
Pram	small dinghy
Quarter	that section of ship between midlength and stern, thus any direction between a right angle to midlength and stern of a ship
Quarter deck	deck above the upper or weather deck extending from the mainmast to the stern, in *Mayflower II* sheltering the great cabin where the 'gentlemen' were accommodated
Running free	sailing with the wind aft
Sheets	lines attached to lower corners (clews) of sails to spread the canvas; sailing into the wind only the lee sheet is hauled aft, the weather sheet left slack
Shrouds	ropes providing lateral support for the masts, crossed with rope 'ratlines' providing steps for sailors to climb the masts
'Splice the mainbrace!'	traditionally a tot of rum for all hands, usually as a reward for good work
Spritsail	sail attached to the bowsprit

Starboard	the right hand side of a ship
Stays	ropes providing fore and aft support for the masts
Stem	the timber at the bow of a ship
Stern	the back, or after end, of a ship
Stiff	a term applied to a ship with a strong righting moment causing it to spring back forcibly when heeled by wind or wave
Stunsail	studding sail; additional sail spread from an extension of a yard to increase the total area of canvas in light winds
Tack (noun)	foremost lower corner of a sail; thus 'on the starboard tack' means sailing with the wind from the starboard side of the ship
Tack (verb)	to turn a sailing ship through the wind ('going about') so that the wind comes on the other side by first turning the bow into the wind
Top	small platform near the head of each mast supporting the heel of the next mast above, and allowing 'topmen' a work station. On *Mayflower II* the tops were round.
Topsail	the sail above the course whose yard is attached to the topmast
Veer	(wind) to change direction clockwise
Way	(nautical) forward movement of a ship
Wear	to turn a sailing ship to the opposite tack by first turning the bow away from the wind
Wind chute	canvas tunnel rigged to air below decks
Windward	direction from which wind is blowing
Yard	timber on which sail is stretched
Yardarm	the end of a yard

BIBLIOGRAPHY

Those wishing for a more detailed knowledge of 17th century sails, rigging and seamanship cannot do better than acquire John Harland's *Seamanship in the Age of Sail* (Conway Maritime Press, 1984)

Mayflower II's designer, the late William A.Baker, published several papers:

Deck Heights in the Early Seventeenth Century, (The American Neptune, vol.XXII, No.2, April 1962);

Early Seventeenth-Century Ship Design (Mayflower Mail Ltd.);

The Arrangement and Construction of Early Seventeenth-Century Ships (Mayflower Mail Ltd.);

The new Mayflower – *including scale Plans and Rigging Specs.* (Barre, 1958)

Accounts of the Mayflower II project and voyage

Charlton, Warwick, *The Voyage of Mayflower II*, Cassell, 1957

Charlton, Warwick, *The Second Mayflower Adventure*, Plimoth Plantation Press, 2007

Padfield, Peter, *The Sea is a Magic Carpet,* Peter Davies, 1959, Thistle Publishing, 2014

Scotney, John, *Brixham's Mayflower*, Brixham Museum, 2019

Villiers, Alan, *Give Me a Ship to Sail*, Hodder & Stoughton, 1958

Printed in Great Britain
by Amazon